HOW
LEADERS
LEARN

HOW LEADERS LEARN

DAVID NOVAK

WITH LARI BISHOP

HARVARD BUSINESS
REVIEW PRESS
BOSTON, MASSACHUSETTS

MASTER THE HABITS OF THE WORLD'S MOST SUCCESSFUL PEOPLE

Library of Congress Cataloging-in-Publication Data

Names: Novak, David, 1953- author.
Title: How leaders learn : master the habits of the world's most successful
   people / David Novak.
Description: Boston, Massachusetts : Harvard Business Review Press, [2024]
| Includes index. |
Identifiers: LCCN 2023053123 (print) | LCCN 2023053124 (ebook)
   | ISBN 9781647827540 (hardcover) | ISBN 9781647827557 (epub)
Subjects: LCSH: Leadership—Case studies. | Chief executive officers—Case
   studies.
Classification: LCC HD57.7 .N683 2024 (print) | LCC HD57.7 (ebook) | DDC
   658.4/092—dc23/eng/20240203
LC record available at https://lccn.loc.gov/2023053123
LC ebook record available at https://lccn.loc.gov/2023053124

ISBN: 978-1-64782-754-0
eISBN: 978-1-64782-755-7

The paper used in this publication meets the requirements of the American National Standard for Permanence of Paper for Publications and Documents in Libraries and Archives Z39.48-1992.

To my amazing grandkids, Audrey, Claire, and Luke.
May you be active learners your whole life through.

And if you want to know the ace up my sleeve,
I've got Wendy.

The most pressing task is
teaching people how to learn.

—Peter Drucker

Contents

The Leaders You'll Learn From

HOW LEADERS LEARN

Introduction

Learn . . . to Discover Possibility

Every successful person I've met in my life—and I've spent time with many of the *most* successful—has learned the discipline of learning. They recognized that it was the only way to expand their potential and the potential of the people around them.

They're like Lara Croft in *Tomb Raider*—probably not where you expected me to go next. When you're playing the game, you can unlock a special survival skill called "Avid Learner." It helps you *earn more experience points* every time you uncover important information in the game. It helps you *advance faster*. I learned this recently when exploring how we talk and think about learning—and it's the perfect explanation of why you need this book, why I'm writing it, and the possibilities it could create for you.

Throughout my life, people have asked if there was a secret to my ability to advance fast in my career, to change the trajectory of teams and companies, and to lead a deeply fulfilling life. The most important thing, I tell them, isn't really a secret. It has always been *learning*. "Become an avid learner!" I would say, long before the *Tomb Raider* developers stole my phrase. No matter what I'm doing or what goal I'm pursuing, learning has always been my default approach to life and work. It has helped me gain more experience faster (like Lara Croft) and helped me survive during the tough times and thrive during the best times. I love working with people to discover great ideas and then use those ideas to create possibility and opportunity.

When you discover how to incorporate learning into all aspects of *your* life, to develop it as a daily discipline and vital skill, you'll grow your career, your leadership, your relationships, and your joy and fulfillment, too. Formal education can help, but the kind of learning I'm talking about doesn't start or end there and it's certainly not dependent on the number of degrees you hold or the pedigree of the schools you attended. I'm speaking from experience. I was a trailer park kid who lived in twenty-three states before high school. I was fortunate to attend college, but I didn't have an Ivy League MBA like many of my colleagues over the years. What I had was an on-the-job, learn-by-doing attitude, and the discipline to stay focused on building this skill. Step by step, I just kept pursuing knowledge, seeking out good ideas, and filling my gaps.

As I advanced in my career, my avid learning gave me access to people, experiences, and environments that I sought out. It gave me access to better insights and greater skill-building, which helped me develop better ideas. It helped me overcome natural biases, be more analytical and more creative, and get better at spotting opportunities and solving problems. It helped me take smarter action. I parlayed those advantages into a career of fast growth that ultimately led me to cofound and lead Yum! Brands, the parent company of KFC, Taco Bell, Pizza Hut, and the Habit Burger, and one of the largest corporations in the world.

When I left my position as CEO after nearly two decades, I had to decide where to focus my time, energy, and experience. What am I going to do? What would help me turn my ideas and plans into a life that brought me energy, excitement, and joy?

With only a little reflection, the answer was obvious: learning.

The great Peter Drucker once wrote, "The most pressing task is teaching people how to learn." I've taken on the challenge of this pressing task in the work I do, and now in this book. Even for people who are naturally curious and interested in solving problems, being an *effective* learner who can turn their learning into *action* takes insight and practice. This book is your practice manual. It's *not* an autobiography. It *is* the collection of wisdom and practical habits from some of the most successful leaders in the world—CEOs from many different industries, military and political leaders, sports greats, experts, and coaches—*and* stories from my own life and career. Chapter by chapter, you'll discover how they've climbed to the highest levels in their respective fields.

Universally, the most successful and happy people and leaders I know, so many of whom you'll be hearing from, operate the same way I do. Learning is their mindset, their differentiating skill, and their approach to life and the world. Now more than ever, with the pace of change in business and the fact that most people change jobs often and even change their careers during their lifetime, a learning discipline isn't just something that's nice to have; it's essential to your success. And when you discover how to master the pursuit of active learning, you'll see the same results in your life and career.

Turning Ideas into Action

When I began working on this book, I realized something was missing in my advice to become an avid learner—advice so core that it had found its way into my books and my leadership development programs. It might work for Lara Croft in a video game, but in the real world, I came to see that it put learning as the end in itself. It can sound like I'm suggesting you become a living, breathing wiki or Siri in human form. But that's not right. Imagine if Tom Brady, one of the most voracious learners I've met, knew everything there was to know about how to throw a football to a teammate down the field but never trained his mind and body to *do* it. Learning by itself isn't enough. You have to focus as much on the action that comes from the learning. So I changed my language. I want to help you become an *active* learner.

An active learner is somebody who seeks out ideas and insights and then pairs them with action and execution. They learn with purpose. The result is greater possibilities—for them and the people around them.

I didn't invent the habit of active learning, but I have invested in understanding how to build it and how to use it, especially by studying the many active learners I've met in my life. These days, I talk with them on my podcast *How Leaders Lead with David Novak*—people like Indra Nooyi, Jack Nicklaus, Junior Bridgeman, Bobbi Brown, Uri Levine, Ginni Rometty, and so many others. They demonstrate a deep commitment to consistent learning followed by action. From their experiences and insights, captured throughout this book, I've discovered three essential building blocks or behaviors:

- They **learn from** anybody and any experience that has something new, interesting, or valuable to offer.

- They **learn to** maintain an open, curious mind and positive relationships (because we learn the most from and with other people).

- And they **learn by** doing the things that need doing or that will make the biggest difference.

So powerful is this model that I've structured the whole book around it. Active learners leverage it to sustain their success, to lead fulfilling lives, and to deepen their connections with other people. Knowing *how* to learn and how to *apply* what they learn are skills they've translated as they moved from one pursuit to another. You'll see them confidently admit that they don't know everything.

You can watch them turn their learning skills inward and use what they find there to coach themselves and grow. And you can identify an active learner by their willingness to tackle new challenges and big problems.

That's how I was able to change lanes and advance faster over the years, moving between roles, functions, and industries without facing too many setbacks or catastrophes. I advanced from a copywriter role at a local ad agency out of college in the mid-1970s to leading a large team serving the Frito-Lay account at a national ad agency. From there, with encouragement from others, I became executive vice president of marketing for Pizza Hut in 1986. I was only thirty-four years old and I didn't have the degrees that many corporate VPs had. PepsiCo owned Pizza Hut at the time, and my active learning skills allowed me to leapfrog from one opportunity to the next at the company. I became executive vice president of marketing for Pepsi-Cola (PepsiCo's beverage division) and then chief operating officer. I was asked to become president of KFC when I was forty-two. The company then added Pizza Hut to my leadership responsibilities. My successful learning and transformation of these companies led to my eventual position as cofounder and president (and eventually CEO) of Yum! Brands in 1997.

I stayed there for two decades. When I left in 2016, I knew I wanted to help more people become great leaders, so I created David Novak Leadership, invested more in the Lift a Life Novak Family Foundation, and launched my podcast. The work we do across these efforts is helping people learn how to uncover important ideas and turn them into actions that change teams, companies, and the world for the better.

All along this journey, I didn't hoard ideas. I spread them. I wanted to help people, teams, and organizations succeed. I've never met a true active learner who didn't feel compelled to share what they learn. And that's why I'm writing this book. I've met so many people who were never taught to be active learners—how to do it or why it matters. It holds them back and prevents them from fulfilling their potential. I want to inspire you to become an active learner and hone the skills that will help you grow and succeed.

How This Book Works

I've organized this book based on the three keys to transforming your learning into action that I mentioned earlier: learn from, learn to, and learn by.

Part one, "Learn From," is devoted to how we can all **learn from the people, environments, and experiences available to us right now.** Active learners don't sit around hoping lessons and ideas will show up on their doorstep. They hunt for learning opportunities wherever they are and whoever they're with so that they can make a positive difference now, not later.

I'm the product of all the learning opportunities shared with me throughout my life, through my upbringing, education, coaching, career moves, friends, family, and more. I have absorbed more from others than one person really deserves. I'm grateful for that every day. But it wasn't only by chance. It was also by choice, a decision I *made* every day that drove the actions I took.

Early on in my career, when I was moving into leadership positions, I used to excuse myself and go to the bathroom every time the people I was with started talking about where they'd earned their business degrees. I never felt like I fit in. (It also didn't help that I looked even younger than my age, which led me to an embarrassing mustache phase.) Eventually though, I realized that the overconfidence that can come from having a specific pedigree can also keep you from being open to ideas and possibilities, wherever they show up or whatever the source.

I'm starting with *learn from* rather than other essential learning skills and habits because if you aren't able to spot opportunities or insights around you, knowing how to learn won't do you much good. You'll read about how Condoleezza Rice learned from her upbringing in segregated Birmingham, and how Patrick Lencioni discovered his "gaps." I'll share how the members of the Dude Perfect team improve their ideas by being truth-tellers, and what Oscar Munoz learned from the United Airlines flight 3411 crisis. These stories and others will reveal that we're all surrounded by ideas just waiting for us to turn into a solution, a fix, a way to grow our careers, a way to help our departments or companies, a way to help our communities, a way to make the world better.

In part two, "Learn To," I'll explore essential **habits for developing open minds and better critical thinking habits, so that you can increase the flow of great ideas into your life** and improve how you analyze them. I'll lead with the most essential skill for learning: listening. How much time do most of us spend really listening, with focus and intention, when people talk to us? How often are we instead multitasking, listening with assumptions, or just thinking about what we're going to have for lunch? Every day, people share great ideas that go nowhere because nobody's *actively* listening. If you can become the one who does listen, you'll have incredible potential for positive impact.

The biggest hurdle most of us face in becoming active learners is our own brain, which creates roadblocks to new ideas. We carry innate biases that we don't always recognize. We like to be right a lot more than we like to be wrong, and our brains are good at convincing us that we are. We tend to focus on the negative, which helps us survive but also shuts us off from opportunity. We can overcome these limitations, though, by asking better questions, checking our judgments, and developing pattern thinking and other behaviors that expand our sphere of influence. As you read along, you'll learn about Jamie Dimon's habits for developing better instincts; how Ken Chenault, former CEO of American Express, overcame the "Ken Zone"; and how Lauren Hobart, CEO of Dick's Sporting Goods, turns to people on the front lines of customer service for the best ideas.

I've mentioned people several times already in this book and we're only a few pages in. You can probably guess that I'm a people person, and I believe that developing people skills and being an active learner go hand in hand. Being curious about, open to, and appreciative of ideas means being curious about, open to, and appreciative of people. It means sharing credit and trusting in their positive intentions. I'll explore those essentials in this part of the book, too.

In part three, "Learn By," we'll explore the nuances of learning by pursuing joy, simplifying, solving problems, prioritizing people, recognizing others on purpose, and much more. **When we learn by doing, we're discovering the insights that come from action.** Some of those insights are about us, some are about others, and some are about the world around us.

Learn by also gives us the greatest opportunities for growth. When we learn by seeking out new challenges, doing the hard things, or teaching what we've learned to others, we stretch ourselves. Instead of incremental growth, we make big leaps in what we know, what we're capable of, and our tolerance for the discomfort that comes from putting ourselves out there—like the time I put myself forward for the chief operating officer role at Pepsi-Cola with almost no operations experience.

Without a formal education in business or marketing (my early career path), I've had to learn by doing, which is the best way to learn. Though I've had some amazing teachers (virtually every boss I've had went on to run a big company, for example), a lot of what I've learned was self-taught. Sometimes, that's the only way to learn. Sometimes there's nobody to ask, no YouTube video to watch, no instruction manual to read. When, for example, Marvin Ellison was the only person at the headquarters of Lowe's who had his experience in the stores or who looked like him, he had to learn to throw his true self forward. You'll also read about why Jim Nantz, award-winning sports commentator, never outsources research and preparation and why Aneel Bhusri, one of the cofounders and CEO of Workday, personally interviewed the first five hundred people the company hired.

The importance of learning by doing is especially true for successful creators and innovators, who are, without exception, active learners.

. . .

When I started out on the journey of writing this book, my editor and I began by learning. We went to school on one of the best-selling books of all time, *How to Win Friends and Influence People* by Dale Carnegie. The book you're reading now is structured a lot like Carnegie's—the chapters are short, driven by stories, and gathered into parts based on an active theme. Because what we learned from Carnegie's example was the power of creating a book that could be read in fifteen-minute increments and deliver something of value and impact with each bite. We learned that it's OK to give people the freedom to read any chapter they feel like reading. You can read straight through or start anywhere you like. And we learned that the best way to deliver insights is through candid stories that move and entertain. So that's what I've tried to do.

Finally, I wrap up each chapter with questions designed to help you turn the big idea into active learning in your own life. As you read on, my hope is that you learn about you—how you learn best, what learning moments have had the biggest impact in your life, and where you have opportunities to grow your learning capacity and capabilities. Self-discovery is the key to acquiring knowledge. I use that term, self-discovery, in two ways: it's the act of learning about yourself and the act of coming up with ideas on your own. Use the questions at the end of the chapters to reflect on what I've shared and then draw your own conclusions or develop your own ideas.

That's really what separates active learners from the rest of the world. They get so excited by the process of learning itself, because they know what they learn will be useful to help them grow. Taking on the role of active learner will lead you to places you never thought you could go. It will reveal possibilities you never imagined. It's as Eric Hoffer, the American philosopher, wrote in *Reflections on the*

Human Condition: "In a time of drastic change, it is the *learners* who inherit the future."[1] They can't wait to discover the next idea, and the next, and the next, because behind every idea is a world of possibility and a brighter future.

I'm excited to see what possibilities this book will bring to your life. Let's see where the first idea takes you.

LEARN FROM

*It's what we learn
after we think we know
it all that counts.*

—humorist Frank McKinney Hubbard . . .
and often repeated by
Coach John Wooden

Chapter 1

Trailer Park University

Learn from your upbringing

My family was one of fifteen attached to the US Coast and Geodetic Survey team. My dad's job was to mark latitudes and longitudes for the nation's mapmakers. The team needed him wherever it needed to make new maps. So, every few months, we'd pack up, hitch our trailers to the back of big government trucks, and move on to a new town so he could mark new latitudes and longitudes. Imagine a circus caravan without the elephants but with the same great sense of anticipation—new terrain to explore, a new lake or stream to swim in.

When people ask me where I'm from, I say, "Well, that's kind of a long story"—because I grew up in trailer parks across the country, wherever my dad had to go. I had lived in twenty-three states by the time I was in seventh grade.

It probably sounds to most of you like a tough way to grow up. I didn't always mind it. The sense of adventure was always there, and because the fifteen families moved together, we took our neighborhood with us, so we had community, even with the constant moving. And *because* of the constant moving—and what that meant for us as kids, leaving friends behind and rarely seeing our own extended families—the families banded together to create a strong infrastructure of support. When I played baseball, for example, about twenty people, extended "family," would show up to watch. Everyone else on the team was lucky to get both their parents there, and I'd have a whole cheering section.

It took me decades to see the connection between those experiences and how I operated in my life and career, especially as a leader. For instance, I didn't understand the influence the support of the survey-team families had on me when I was a kid because it was my "normal." But it made me feel cared for, appreciated, and special, and I learned that making other people feel that way was one of the most significant things I could do in life. Showing my support for and recognition of people, their good work, their ideas, became my guiding star.

In her great book *Insight*, Tasha Eurich writes about the critical skill of self-awareness and how to build it. She explains that self-aware people understand their values, aspirations, passions, the environments where they are happiest, their patterns of behavior, their reactions, and the effect they have on others. Throughout this book, I'll come back to some of these elements, because one of the most powerful things we can learn in life is who we are. Our upbringings are gold mines of information, though, so why not start there?

Our upbringings shape us—the good and bad experiences, the normal experiences of our day-to-day lives. **When you choose to *learn from your upbringing*, you learn who you are, your strengths and weaknesses, your unique perspective, and your blind spots.**

Being an active learner means being a historian of your own life, so start by reflecting on your past, beginning with your earliest experiences and influences. Hunt for insights about what you value, how you think, and what biases you might hold. You might discover why you feel affinity toward certain people or ideas. All of this self-knowledge will expand your capacity for learning in the present.

There are many ways to do this historical scan. One I like comes from psychologist Dan McAdams, who has focused most of his research and work on what our life stories can tell us about who we are. He helped develop a technique called the "Guided Autobiography," asking people to identify important events in their lives and then asking thought-provoking questions about those events. The most revealing questions are:

- "Why do you think this is an important event in your life story?"

- "What does this event say about who you are, who you were, who you might be, or how you have developed over time?"[1]

I've done a similar exercise throughout my life as a leader, sketching my lifeline, including the important experiences and the high points and low points. Next to each critical experience, I note the impact it had on me and what I learned. This process has taught me that I have not succeeded in life *in spite of* my nomadic upbringing; I've succeeded *because* of it. Being born in the United States to loving and supporting parents, Charles and Jean Novak, was my biggest break in life. Next to my high point of being raised by my mom and dad, I write "mentor and coach." My dad was my first *coach*, and my mother was my first *mentor*.

Having my community in the stands during games mattered, but my parents played the biggest role in developing my focus on people. They modeled what it looked like to be a good coach and mentor, and they emphasized the importance of building relationships early and often. Even as an older adult, every time I was a guest commentator on CNBC's *Squawk Box*, they would watch and then call and tell me how great I did.

I remember how, every time we arrived in a new town, my mother would take me to the local school and say, "Look, David, you've got to take the initiative to make friends. Don't hang back and wait for the other kids to come to you. We're only going to be here for a few months, so make them count." With her advice and our nomadic life, I learned that you were only ever one friend away from happiness. I carried that idea with me into every new work environment throughout my career.

Of course, that didn't entirely take away my anxiety of going in cold to a new school, but it did help me walk through the fear and get on with it. Once there, what made all the difference was the first person to acknowledge me in some way, the first kid to be brave enough to say hi or ask where we had come from. I learned that anybody who tries to make others feel more comfortable in a new situation is generally a good human being, and I've tried to be that person for others whenever possible, especially in my leadership roles.

I don't want to make my childhood sound idyllic. We certainly struggled sometimes and in some towns. We weren't wealthy; we had to work hard for the things we had. My father left us a few summers to take higher-paying and more dangerous jobs in remote places, like the wilds of Alaska. Few important stories from our lives are straightforward or simple, all good or all bad. Recognizing that is something Tasha Eurich highlights as an important sign of self-awareness in her book: "Self-aware people tend to knit more complex narratives of their key life events: they are more likely to describe each event from different perspectives, include multiple explanations, and explore complex and even contradictory emotions. . . . Instead of searching for simple, generalizable facts, **self-aware people appreciate the complicated nature of the key events in their lives**. Perhaps for this reason, complex life stories are associated with continued personal growth and maturity years into the future."[2] I've seen this same kind of nuanced storytelling, or self-awareness, from so many of the active learners I've met when they talk about their upbringings.

Indra Nooyi, the former CEO of PepsiCo, told me a story of learning from her mother to be both aspirational and competitive. When she was young, her mother gave Indra and her siblings a task at dinner. For example, she'd say, "Give me a speech about what you would do if you were the prime minister of the country." At the end of dinner, when they had all given their speeches, her mother chose the best speech and handed out the prize—a *tiny* piece of chocolate. Her mother never tried to make sure that every kid won at least once or give the prize in turns. Every time, she gave the chocolate to the person who had delivered the *best* speech. Reflecting on this, Indra said, "Today, you give me a bar of chocolate, a *giant* bar of chocolate, and it doesn't taste as good as that tiny, tiny bit of chocolate."

The stories James Gorman, CEO of Morgan Stanley, shared of learning from his father's raised bar are funnier—at least from a distance of a few decades—but helped him develop a deep sense of both humility and independence. He is an Australian who grew up as one of ten children. "What it teaches you is that you're not that special," he said. "There's somebody who's smarter, somebody who's more athletic, somebody who's funnier, somebody who's better looking." And then there's his father. His methods might not align with modern parenting advice, but they certainly made James both humble and self-reliant when it came to his own success. When James was young, his father gave all the kids an IQ test and then posted the results on the living room door, in order. Next to each, he listed their likely career potential. Next to James's middling score, he wrote "middle management." His father also made it clear that all the kids would support themselves financially from the moment they turned eighteen, including figuring out how to pay for college. James worked three jobs while getting his degree, including cleaning the toilets in his dorm.

Condoleezza Rice will tell you that she has a positive perspective on her upbringing, despite the fact that it came with more challenges than most people's. "I always say something that's maybe a little bit paradoxical, which is that I'm actually glad I grew up in segregated Birmingham," she told me. She was nine years old when the Civil Rights Act passed. Before then, she lived in a small community full of adults, many of whom were schoolteachers, who sent two clear messages: First, you're going to have to be twice as good to succeed in a segregated environment. Second, you may not be able to control your circumstances, but you can control your response to those circumstances. If you respond as a victim, then you have given control of your life over to someone else. "Those two lessons . . . were a kind of armor in their way of preparing us for what they thought was likely to be a very hostile world for a long time to come. . . . If there's a barrier, you go around it, over it, or through it, but you don't let it stop you. I learned that in the circumstances of segregated Birmingham, and I'm grateful because I took those lessons into life with me."

Those lessons of both self-respect *and* personal responsibility influenced how she responded to challenging circumstances. She began her career as a Soviet military specialist and was a unique presence in a lot of rooms. She tried to make being included a two-way street, their responsibility and hers. She quickly showed people that she belonged there, but she also made the effort to bring down the potential tension level. As a young professor, she got a one-year fellowship to work for the strategic nuclear planning division of the Joint Chiefs of Staff. "I was three things they had never seen," she told me. "Female, black, and civilian. . . . The first day they said, 'The rookie makes the coffee.' Now I could have said, 'I'm a professor at Stanford. I don't make coffee.' I made the coffee. The truth is I make coffee so strong, nobody can drink it. They never asked me again. It lowered the temperature. And then the next week, I won the football pool. Now we had something to talk about on Monday mornings. And pretty soon, I was just real comfortable with them, and they were real comfortable with me."

What about the stories you tell from your life and your upbringing? Have you mined them for the deeper, more complex insights into who you are and how you think and behave? Have you learned about your strengths and blind spots? If you haven't, you may be limiting what you can learn now. You may be at risk of repeating patterns that don't serve you well.

For instance, so much of my unusual childhood would serve me well in life, but it especially contributed to one of my greatest strengths, which is being comfortable with and excited about change. But it could also be a weakness if I let it blind me to the fact that not every-body approaches the world in the same way. On my résumé, you'll see one example of this. I changed jobs often. I was always looking for the next growth opportunity and I never thought twice about packing up the proverbial trailer and moving to the next site. That sensibility, paired with my ambition, contributed to my career success, but you're not going to make everybody happy when you move in and out of jobs. Even though I grew up with a strong focus on people and relationships, I have also blindly assumed that those around me were ready to jump into the truck and head to the next town, too, without taking their feelings into consideration.

One of the most important roles of my career was senior vice president of marketing for Pizza Hut. After more than a decade working for outside agencies, it was my first job inside a large company. Steve Reinemund, president of Pizza Hut, took a chance and hired me despite the fact that I had no experience in the restaurant industry. He championed me from day one and took the time to teach me everything he knew about the business, which was a lot. His risk and investment paid off, though. Over three years I helped double sales and profits and turn around the delivery business.

Because of my team's success, Roger Enrico, CEO of PepsiCo Worldwide Beverages, asked me to come over to the beverage division as executive vice president of marketing and sales. It was a big move, because everybody knew how core the beverage division was to the company. And it was a great learning opportunity. It also meant leaving Wichita, Kansas, for New York, a hotbed of networking and career opportunities. I jumped at the chance.

Probably a little too quickly.

Steve Reinemund at Pizza Hut wasn't happy; he didn't have an obvious replacement for me. I didn't involve him much in my discussions with Roger Enrico, and even though he had been a wonderful coach and mentor, I didn't seek his counsel as I was considering the move. He wasn't in the dark about the situation, but I handed him the decision as a done deal. He had given me the biggest break in my career, and I owed him a lot more sensitivity than I had given him. I simply wasn't aware enough that the kind of ease with change and moving on I had developed all the way back in elementary school wasn't innate to everyone. It took us a while to reestablish our great relationship after that, and it took years for me to learn that I had to slow down, not get ahead of myself, and make sure I put myself in other people's shoes.

. . .

Our biggest influences may have been our parents, teachers, coaches, friends, social workers, an entire community, or society. We may have had easier upbringings or tougher upbringings. No matter who or what influenced us in the past, we can learn from those experiences— because the best gift any of us can give ourselves is to know thyself.

Learning from Your Upbringing

- Who in your life has had the greatest impact on your values, goals, worldview, confidence?

- Map the peaks and valleys in your lifeline. What can you learn from each?

- What's one story from your early years that proves what you're capable of when you take a learning perspective?

Chapter 2

Learn from new environments

Unstuck Yourself

Throughout my career, even if I didn't always know where I was headed, I did know that I wanted to keep growing, to keep improving. Usually, that meant seeking out new environments. I recognize that my unique upbringing—moving into a new town and new school every few months until I was twelve—probably made me more comfortable with this kind of change than many, but in my experience, most active learners follow a similar pattern, because *not* moving means not *growing*.

New environments bring uncertainty and risk, two things humans really don't like. The brain weighs threats of loss heavier than it does opportunities for gain. Whether it's a move to a new city or a move to a new company, we don't know the people or the culture and we don't know if we'll succeed when we get there. The brain tells us it's best if we just stay where we are, in our more certain, less risky, known environment. But that's not always the right choice. Josh Waitzkin, child chess prodigy, subject of the book and movie *Searching for Bobby Fischer*, and later a tai chi world champion, wrote in *The Art of Learning*, "Growth comes at the expense of previous comfort or safety."[1]

Active learners feel discomfort in new environments, too, but they overcome their natural risk-avoidance tendencies by focusing on the opportunities for growth. **For active learners, atrophy is more uncomfortable than change.** That mindset helps them *find* things to learn and *use* what they learn, which makes them more successful in a new environment. When they eventually stop growing and learning in that environment, they know it's time to look for a new opportunity.

One way they reduce the sense of risk and build enough confidence to take a leap is to assess and choose new environments carefully. You can do the same. When looking at a new environment, evaluate it for these four sources of learning:

- New knowledge, skills, or systems

- New ideas and innovative thinking

- New people and their perspectives and opinions

- New influences that lead to personal growth

Just because an environment is new doesn't mean it will be ideal, *especially* when it comes to opportunities to learn. For example, I experienced at least three new schools a year until I was in middle school. Some were amazing, others weren't. At one school, I was bullied every day. At another, I had a teacher who invested in me even though I would only be there a short time. I learned to read rooms quickly over the years, and in my professional life, that made a big difference in how I chose the places I worked, picking environments I knew would be worth the risk.

After college, my first job was with a small, local advertising agency. After a couple of years and some incredible learn-by-doing experience, I was ready to grow my skills *and* shift to client management. I wanted to work at a bigger company that would attract more national clients and more talented people. I sent out twenty-five résumés to the top twenty-five agencies in the country and was offered a position at Ketchum, McLeod, & Grove in Pittsburgh as an account manager, a big step up. There I worked for Tom James, who knew as much about marketing as anyone and who taught me everything he knew. After a couple of years at Ketchum, though, I felt ready to go even bigger. With Tom's help, I got interviews with a few large agencies in the advertising mecca of New York, exactly what I had been hoping for.

This was the moment that I began to realize that **some new environments aren't going to advance your learning; they might even slow you down.** In New York, I felt out of place. I sensed that the agencies saw just a kid from a Midwest state school with *only* a bachelor's degree. I was interviewing with people who had MBAs, many from Ivy League schools. They seemed so pedigree driven that I suspected no one was going to chance letting me work on their big, high-profile accounts. I knew what I was capable of, but if I took a job with one of those agencies, I wasn't sure I would get the opportunity to prove it. I wasn't going to be playing in the big leagues, at least not in a way that would advance my learning fast.

Luckily, a better environment showed itself. An agency in Dallas called Tracy Locke was looking for someone to work on its Frito-Lay account, running the campaign for a new product: Tostitos. It was a highly visible, national packaged goods account, where I could learn the most sophisticated marketing and advertising strategies. It felt like the right new environment for me. It was—and it catapulted me forward in my career.

So, how do you choose a new environment that will do the same for you, or will catapult you in some other way? First, **make sure the new environment will offer opportunities to learn and grow** in any area that's important to you right now, like I did. This is especially true when you have an ambition but aren't sure how to get there. You can follow tech CEO and entrepreneur Sukhinder Singh Cassidy's advice on what she calls the power of proximity: "When attempting to plot out the future, we'll often perform desk research to learn how others have achieved something similar to what we want. . . . As important as this work is, the next important step is to insert ourselves in an environment filled with people who routinely do what we're struggling to imagine."[2] This is the whole point of choosing a new environment.

Second, **choose an environment that's suited to you.** Understanding your personal ideal environment is an important aspect of self-awareness. You can develop it by taking the time to consider what kinds of environments help you thrive and what kinds of environments make you so uncomfortable it's hard to focus on learning. It's one reason everybody should learn as much as they can about the culture of a company before accepting a job. The question you're trying to answer is, Is this the kind of environment that will help me be happy and successful and focused on growth—or not? The right environment for you may not always be the one you're *supposed* to inhabit. New York at that time in my career wasn't right for me, although any number of people would have told me it was where I needed to be.

Of course, the answer to what environment is suited to you isn't always obvious even after reflection. Take Carol Loomis's experience in deciding to move to New York to work for *Fortune* magazine. Despite coming from a small town in the Midwest—graduating in a class of thirty-six—Loomis's impression of working for a high-powered company in New York was the opposite of mine. She knew she wanted that before she had even graduated from one of the highest-regarded journalism schools in the country, the University of Missouri in Columbia. New York was home base for three big magazines—*Life*, *Time*, and *Fortune*. It wasn't long before she got in the door at *Fortune*.

New York was the environment with the best opportunities for a business journalist. But that didn't make it easy for a woman in the fifties and sixties, when Carol was starting out. "*Fortune*, like the rest of the Time Inc. magazines, had been set up in the way that [founder] Henry Luce thought the world should be run," Carol told me. "And that was that men wrote and women helped them." For many people, that would be a big, waving red flag. Despite being hired in a support role as a researcher, though, Carol loved the job. She traveled all over the country with the senior writers and sat in on their interviews.

It was an incredible *learning* experience. "I had no false assumptions about how much I knew," she said. She was promoted quickly into the position of assistant chief of research, and eventually—after eight years with *Fortune*—she finally got the opportunity to write. "I had not been impatient all that time. . . . I felt all that time that I was learning."

She ended up working for *Fortune* for sixty years, constantly finding new environments within the company to explore. She helped oversee the creation of the *Fortune* 500 list (because she loved numbers), became an expert in corporate finance (she coined the term *hedge fund*), and became the longtime editor of Warren Buffett's annual letter to shareholders (they're good friends and speak almost every day). When Carol officially retired in 2014, Warren said, "At eighty-five, she is interested in learning more."

Despite how it might have seemed on the surface, *Fortune* was the perfect environment for Carol. Sometimes, you have to dig deep and figure out your priorities as you're choosing the environment that will help you grow.

Third, **choose an environment that will exert the right influences on you,** so that you're not only learning new skills, new knowledge, and new ideas, but also absorbing better collaboration, better leadership, better self-management, or whatever area of personal growth you think you need to work on. Our social and cultural environments have a huge impact on our thinking and behavior. In *Influencer*, psychologist Joseph Grenny and his coauthors explain that if you want to change behavior, you have to make changes to the social and structural environment. In *Atomic Habits*, James Clear argues that our environments usually matter more than our motivation when it comes to building new habits: "Especially over a long time period, your personal characteristics tend to get overpowered by your environment."[3]

You can either fight that truth or leverage it to learn more and grow more. Eric Gleacher recognized the power of environment and how it could not only offer new skills but also shape the person he would

become at a surprisingly young age. After graduating from North-
western University, he voluntarily enrolled in the Marine Corps, one
year before the Vietnam era draft began. He said, "I decided that if I
was going to do it, I was going to do it right. . . . If I'm going to serve,
I'm going to do the most challenging thing available. And that was the
Marines." He signed up with the idea, *Let's see if I can cut it.*

His first assignment after training at Quantico—a leadership
assignment because he was a college graduate—was to the fleet
marine force, second marine division, at Camp Lejeune, North
Carolina. When he arrived, his platoon was out in the field training and wouldn't be back for a few days. A sergeant told him to
review files to learn about the men in his platoon. He was immediately intimidated. Half of them were highly experienced, serving
offshore during the Cuban Missile Crisis. "What am I going to do
here?" he wondered. "I'm supposed to be the superior officer. I'm
twenty-three years old. I got through the training at Quantico, but
this is really serious."

He decided his only option was to be himself, dive in, and do what
he was supposed to do. Within three or four months in that environment, he told me, he learned everything that would be important to
him for the rest of his career and life, deep values that influenced how
he led, how he raised his children, how he treated people.

"I learned that you had to deal with people with flawless integrity.
Anything short of that when dealing with marine infantry troops,
you could forget about it. It had to be the truth." He learned to pursue
excellence in everything he did. This was before elite training programs like the Navy SEALs existed. The marines were the elite, and
that meant a lot to the men. "If you went out to the rifle range, you
had to try to be the top shooter. Whatever you tried to do, you had to
pursue excellence." And he learned a value and a talent for treating
people equally. His son, Jimmy, once described it this way in a book
dedication: "He talks to doormen with the same respect as he does
a CEO." The diversity of the forty-five men in his troop was vast. Most
hadn't graduated from high school, he told me, but they were smart

as hell, intuitive, and wanted to be the best. "I gained that breadth of knowledge about people, and it affected me forever."

After he left the marines, Eric leveraged these lessons as he earned his MBA and eventually moved into the mergers and acquisitions business. He founded the M&A department at Lehman Brothers, was the head of that department at Morgan Stanley, and then founded his own successful firm. He's a legend in the industry. None of that would have been possible without the values and ideals and leadership traits he absorbed in the Marine Corps.

Eric sought out a new environment and chose it carefully. What he learned in it profoundly influenced the rest of his life. That's what the right environment can do for any of us. For instance, we all know people who are old at twenty-seven and people who are young at eighty-eight. The people who stay young their whole lives are the active learners. And exploring new environments—especially environments that are future focused—is one way they stay young. When I was leaving Yum! Brands as CEO, I had many new environments offered to me. I was asked to join all sorts of corporate boards. I said no to most, but I said yes to joining the board of Comcast. It was an industry I did not know much about, *and* it was heavy on technology and new forms of media. I knew that just by being on the board, listening to the conversations, and hearing from the company's leaders, I'd constantly learn about the most current ideas in media and tech. And it has worked! I can tell you I know a lot more than most people my age about Netflix, Hulu, Harry Potter, Nintendo, what it takes to make a hit movie like *Oppenheimer*.

If you're still hesitant to make a move that you think is probably a good idea, you can be proactive in tackling your anxiety. Ryan Serhant, bestselling author, founder of one of the most successful real estate brokerages in the United States, and the star of *Million Dollar Listing*, doesn't come to new environments comfortably. He talked to me about being a shy kid with little confidence. His choice to pursue acting and then high-profile real estate and media might seem unusual. To be successful in either, he has pushed himself into environments and situations that weren't comfortable but that he knew would help him learn and grow. He's developed a technique to help him overcome anxiety in a new environment. He pulls out his phone and writes a pro-con list for his situation, focused on what is making him most nervous and what good could come from it. For example, he'll do it before walking into an event he's never attended and doesn't know anybody but that gives him an opportunity to meet potential clients. Writing down the list of reasons that an environment or situation could be bad offers powerful learning. "If you looked at it tomorrow," Ryan said in our conversation, "you'd laugh and be angry that you didn't take advantage of the situation," because our fears are usually unfounded and can seem almost trivial after the fact. The list of all the good things that could come is what really helps calm his nerves.

Despite the work your brain does to keep you safe from the unknown, you can learn to overcome the barriers. The risks of staying where you are, standing still, and missing out on all the learning and potential of a new environment, chosen carefully, are almost always worse than the risks of making the move.

Learning from New Environments

- Have you ever stayed in an environment—a team, a company, an apartment, a city—longer than you should have? What happened when you finally moved to a new one?

- What are you learning right now from your environment? Is it time to move on?

- Consider the characteristics of the environments where you have learned and grown the most, things like pace, culture, leadership approach, and more. How can you hunt for those traits as you choose your next move?

Chapter 3

Learn from people who know what you don't

Fill Your Gaps

One of the biggest leaps I made in my career was moving from chief *marketing* officer to chief *operating* officer for PepsiCo's beverage division. I literally had to beg for the role—because I had zero operations experience. To seal the deal, I told the CEO that if I wasn't succeeding in six months, he could move me back into marketing with no argument from me, or even fire me.

It was a risky offer. As the head of marketing, I rarely visited operational centers like bottling plants. And when I did, I'd always listen politely to the tour guides and managers and nod as though I was absorbing what they shared. Really, the information would just bounce off my invisible marketing helmet.

If I was going *prove* that I was succeeding in operations in just six months, I had to fill my knowledge gaps *fast*. Luckily, I had discovered an essential tactic for doing that: The secret to fast-tracking knowledge and confidence, a secret every active learner I know leverages, is to **first identify and acknowledge your gaps. Then, find the right experts and ask them as many questions as possible.** They know what you don't, and usually they're happy to help.

I started by assembling people who knew the bottling processes inside and out, who knew how to solve supply chain problems and how to control costs and increase profits. Then, I found the people I thought would know the most about the problems in our operations and good solutions to the problems.

Those people, of course, are the ones making the product and talking to the customers. I developed a routine: Go to a city with a bottling plant. Get up at 5 a.m., talk to the route salespeople before they left, and listen carefully to their answers to my questions: "What are we hearing from our customers? What are we doing well? What do we need to do better?" Sometimes, I would go on sales calls with them to ask customers the same questions. Back at the bottling plant, I'd do the same with the people on the line and on the floor.

Through them, I learned so much. Our forecasting was terrible, and we constantly ran out of stock. We couldn't get product out of the warehouse fast enough. Morale was lousy. Day by day, one tour after another, I turned to people who I thought knew more than I did, and probably more than my team of executives did, to help fill the gaps in my knowledge.

When I debriefed managers of the plants, they were often surprised. They would ask, "How did you find this out so fast?" And I'd say, "I asked."

It's amazing what you can learn when you ask people who know more than you to share their knowledge. Sometimes you need to put them at ease or make it safe for them to tell you the truth (more on that in the next chapter), but generally they *want* to share, and they love it when somebody listens. It's also the fastest way to insight. You skip over trial and error. You leapfrog over the stuff others have already figured out. And that allows you to get to the heart of an issue, a problem, an opportunity, much faster.

Maritza Montiel, who is on the Comcast board of directors with me, used those strategies to dramatically grow the well-known professional services firm Deloitte, even before she became the deputy CEO and vice chair. One of her great successes was to quickly develop and grow an entirely new line of business—consulting for the federal government.

She recognized the massive opportunity of linking up with one of the biggest buyers of professional services in the world. She researched it and then presented her ideas to the board. Another managing partner at the company approached her after and said, "This will never work. We've tried doing this, and it will never work." But it did. Today, Deloitte is one of the largest providers of professional services to the federal government, and the business has become crucial to the company.

Maritza will tell you, though, that she was very clear about her gaps. "I certainly didn't know anything about doing business with the federal government." The first thing she did was recruit a partner who did. Together, they built a team full of talent and experience. "If you're going to be effective and successful, you need to surround yourself with people who are smarter than you," she told me.

For some people, that can be a hard thing to admit, and in Maritza's case, I imagine it could be especially difficult. She was a female leader operating in a predominantly male-led industry and company. She was only the sixth woman to reach partner at Deloitte and the first Latina. And she's a Cuban immigrant who grew up as one of three children to a single mom. Those experiences might make anybody striving to succeed in this environment more prone to focus on proving what they know rather than acknowledging what they don't. But Maritza is an active learner.

To spot their gaps, active learners ask questions like, "Where do I need help to accomplish my goal?" and "What could derail me?" Sometimes the answers are reasonably obvious, like they were for me and Maritza. Sometimes our gaps are harder to spot without a nudge or some help.

Patrick Lencioni found his gaps trickier to manage when a colleague asked him, kindly, "Why are you like this?" She told him she noticed he showed up in the morning excited for the day but would suddenly turn into a grump in the middle of a meeting. Then, in the next meeting, he would be upbeat again. He recognized it himself, and it bothered him, but he could never figure out why he was hot and cold. His colleague asked the question with curiosity and compassion, and that helped him say, "I don't know, but I want to figure it out." Together, they dug in. For four hours, they analyzed the kinds of work he did (and many of us do) throughout the day. They identified six "getting things done" talents, what they called working geniuses:

- Wonder: considering possibility, potential, and opportunity

- Invention: creating novel ideas or solutions

- Discernment: evaluating and analyzing ideas and situations

- Galvanizing: organizing and inspiring others to take action

- Enablement: providing encouragement and assistance

- Tenacity: pushing projects to completion

Patrick knew he was strong in two of them: invention and discernment. And when he thought about the others, he wasn't as happy or energized. He tested this model with others, at work and at home, and the results proved astounding. One CEO got teary: "Now I know what's wrong," he said. Patrick and his team created an assessment—more than half a million people have taken it—and wrote a book, *The 6 Types of Working Geniuses*. It's helping people understand where they can turn to others for help and support.

Patrick thinks it's more powerful and life changing than anything he's done. "Now I know what I'm good at," he told me. "I know what I suck at. And I can celebrate it better. I have a way to build teams where people are leaning into each other's strengths and filling in each other's gaps."

You can check out Patrick's assessment or another one, like CliftonStrengths, DISC, Myers-Briggs, and so on. There are quite a few, and they tend to overlap. You don't have to do them all, but doing a couple could help you gather a few insights about yourself. Every time you learn about a strength or a foundational behavior or trait, you're also identifying your gaps that others can help you fill.

When you're trying to identify the people who know more than you, test your assumptions about experts. You don't need the most elite, celebrated, or successful person in a field. An expert is simply somebody who knows a lot about something—and you can find those people in any number of places and positions.

For example, John Weinberg is a legend in the finance world and head of Goldman Sachs for almost fifteen years. He was one of the first people I heard talk about filling gaps, but it had nothing to do with business. He was a marine during World War II, but maybe not what you're picturing in your mind. He was five feet seven and not exactly athletic. He wasn't great with his rifle. He made it through basic training, but so did most guys at the time. He took a hard look at his odds and doubted whether he could keep himself alive through the war. John wasn't useless—he was well educated and well-liked. His gear was always well organized and well cared for. He was a good thinker and didn't get rattled easily. So, he went to a soldier who knew what John didn't know about soldiering and made him a deal: "If you can help keep me alive, teach me how to protect myself, and shoot and not get shot, I'll help you take care of your gear and help you in any other way I can." His brother-in-arms agreed, and month by month, John became a better soldier. "He filled my gaps," John told me. He also saved his life more than once.

Often, I gathered more essential knowledge from people on the front lines—team members on the bottling line, in the warehouse, or working the fryer at KFC—than I did the executives. They knew things we didn't, pointed out critical problems, and helped me understand why our latest, greatest idea wasn't going to work in practice the way we thought.

Every company is filled with experts. No matter the question, the answer is almost always in the building. If you need to understand the company's history, meet with a twenty-five-year veteran. If you want to know what customers are thinking, talk to customer service. If you can't get delivery trucks out on time, hop on a route with a delivery person.

But I also look outside the building quite often. When I'm trying to solve specific challenges, I rarely hire consultants, instead opting for an accredited expert—an established business figure, a highly experienced practitioner, or the author of a well-received book on the subject.

My wife, Wendy, has lived with type 1 diabetes since she was a child. So through the Lift a Life Novak Family Foundation, led by our daughter, Ashley Butler, we established the Wendy Novak Diabetes Institute at our local medical center. We want to make it one of the top of its kind in the country. It has been a huge undertaking. From funding to science, it was totally new territory for us. There was *quite* a lot that we didn't know. Even the endocrinologist who leads the institute was new to this kind of work.

We turned to the best experts we could find, bringing in medical leaders from the Barbara Davis Center for Diabetes in Colorado, one of the best in the country. We spent a day touring its facilities and interviewing the administrators. How do they run the place? How do they stay on top of innovations in care and provide great patient experiences? We visited St. Jude Children's Research Hospital and learned how to create space that caters to children. I remember even simple lessons, like when they mentioned how all colors of paint essentially cost the same, so choose bright, happy, inviting colors.

We brought the hospital's proposal for how we could integrate the institute into their facility to people I know who have created foundation-funded medical centers. Those experienced, knowledgeable people helped us understand the questions we should ask and how to communicate our goals and requirements. Conversation by conversation, we felt more confident that we could do what we had planned and that we were making good decisions, because we just kept filling our gaps.

If you're wondering who you should turn to, always **start with people who have applied their ideas in the real world** and can prove that they work. At Yum! I turned to people like Jim Collins, Larry Bossidy, Howard Schultz, and Noel Tichy. Here's a tip: when I brought these experts in to help us tackle a challenge, I never asked them to deliver their usual stump speech. I included as many of our leaders as possible in the meeting, and then we did a Q&A. Or we asked them to train us on specific practices and tools. We weren't trying to absorb broad or general wisdom. We had a purpose to what we wanted to learn, and a Q&A or actual exercises were much more valuable than a speech.

Next, **ask, Will they actually fill my gaps, or will they hold back their best ideas** or try to elevate their ego by making what they know seem complex and hard to understand? Will they make their knowledge simple and clear? Essentially, you're asking, Is this person an active learner? Because active learners love helping people fill their gaps.

One of the best experts—the best teachers—I've met is Warren Buffett. When I became CEO of Yum! Brands, my greatest *personal* knowledge gap was the financials of a publicly traded company and dealing with Wall Street analysts and investors. I had taken some courses, but I knew that basic knowledge wouldn't be enough to manage the nuances. I was lucky to have access to the guru himself, so I traveled to Omaha and spent a couple of hours with him, eating lunch at KFC. (Whenever we did, he always salted his original recipe chicken, something not many people would do, and he always took a photo with the team at the restaurant.)

Warren gave me the best advice I ever got about communicating with these groups, who honestly intimidated me. At one point, he asked, "David, you're so passionate about your brands, but do you ever talk about what's wrong or what could go wrong?" Tell investors and analysts that you're in a tough business, he said, and remind them that you aren't going to be successful every quarter. You'll win in the long run because you're building the business the right way. He told me that if I addressed the things that could go wrong, over time they would trust that I was looking at our business in a balanced way. And that's what I did. Because Warren Buffett taught me the concept of sober selling, I became much more confident and trustworthy with investors and analysts.

It also helped that Jamie Dimon, who is now CEO of JPMorgan Chase, joined the board. He was obviously a high-level finance guy—and he's an active learner. One of the key reasons he agreed to be on the board *was to learn from me and others* about the consumer side of a retail business, because that was his gap. He wanted a better understanding of how to improve customer satisfaction, customer relations, and customer engagement, and he thought he could develop it by tapping into our knowledge.

A final tip: **if you want people to share their know-how with you, you need to spread know-how.** You need to be willing to share with them, too. We'll talk more about this in coming chapters.

If you want to be an active learner, I suggest you assume that others know more than you about something. Learn from them every day. You'll suddenly see shortcuts to the goals you're trying to accomplish or the solutions you're trying to develop. You'll feel like a kid again, full of curiosity and inspiration. And when it's time for you to make a decision and take action, you can do it with the confidence that comes only from expert-level insights.

Learning from People Who Know What You Don't

- Is there a place in your life where you're stuck? Have you turned to somebody who knows more than you to help you figure out how to move forward? Who could that person be?

- What experts in your life and career have made the biggest difference? What are some of the traits they shared?

- Are you limiting your definition of "expert"? Or are you overlooking an expert in your life, somebody who knows what you don't but who you haven't tapped to help you fill a gap?

Learn from your truth-tellers

Chapter 4
You've Got Something in Your Teeth

When I lobbied to be both the chairman and CEO of Yum! Brands, a new company that was being created to house PepsiCo's restaurant businesses, Roger Enrico said to me, "David, you don't know what you don't know." I didn't like that. I had successfully led Pizza Hut and KFC through some tough times as president of both, and I thought I was ready to level up to a massive, publicly traded company that would include those companies plus Taco Bell.

Roger believed I could run the company, but also thought I needed a seasoned chairman, a partner who could balance my strengths and areas for growth. As someone who had spent decades rising to the role of chairman and CEO of PepsiCo, along the way hiring the right leaders to run regions and divisions, Roger was probably right. Still, I didn't see it, and I kept fighting for the role I wanted.

Roger wasn't going to back down, but I did get one concession from him: I could recommend a chairman. I suggested the whip-smart Andy Pearson, a tough boss and business guru with nearly fifty years of experience. Andy had been the president of PepsiCo and was at the helm when the company acquired Taco Bell and Pizza Hut. We would cofound Yum! Brands together, him as chairman and CEO and me as vice chairman and president.

Andy once told me a story that captured how he had become so successful, so respected. After leaving PepsiCo, he was a hot commodity, but he decided to take a break from corporate leadership. Instead, he would bring his vast knowledge to the lucky students at Harvard Business School. Every insight he could squeeze into a ninety-minute lecture on exactly how to lead a company would be eagerly captured by the MBAs. Seemed straightforward.

At the end of his first semester, he handed out the requisite student evaluation forms without much thought. Of course, the students would be grateful for everything they had learned. Imagine his surprise when the dean of the school told him he was literally the worst-rated professor at the entire university. "They said I wasn't teaching," he told me. "I was preaching."

Andy could have written it off or made some minor adjustments to his approach. He could have said, "Teaching is not for me." But that wasn't Andy. Instead, he acknowledged that maybe he didn't know as much about teaching MBA students as he thought and dug into the feedback. There he found that students wanted less lecturing and more discussion. Fewer of his stories and more cases they could analyze together. Less of his voice and more from his incredible network of experienced business leaders.

Andy gathered ideas from these truth-tellers and took action. He changed *everything* about how he taught. The next year, the students evaluated him as the best teacher at the school.

Andy taught me more about how to keep learning and growing than anyone. Over time, he became my best friend, like a mentor, a second father, and a brother all rolled into one. And he became one of my truth-tellers.

Truth-tellers are a great source of learning in our lives. But too often, we don't take advantage of them because we can't handle the truth. We don't like to hear "Investors don't believe you're ready to run this multibillion-dollar global business on your own," or "You're a terrible teacher," or even "You've got something in your teeth." It's as the French philosopher and art critic Denis Diderot once said, "We swallow greedily any lie that flatters us, but we sip only little by little at a truth we find bitter."

It's not just philosophy; it's how we're wired. Neurologically, we process social pain in almost the same way that we process physical pain—as a threat to eliminate.[1] When somebody tells us a less than positive truth about us, our performance, or our brilliant ideas, we process it as a threat to our status, sense of fairness, or relationship with the teller. Studies have even shown that social rejection can lead to inflammation in the body.[2]

When somebody cares enough and is brave enough to tell you the truth, your best course of action is to fight your instincts to dismiss it or hide from it. Overcome your brain's biological drive to protect you. Shut down the voice in your head telling you they're wrong. Don't run out of the room. Take some deep calming breaths (that really works), remind yourself that this person probably has a good reason for bringing the truth to your attention, and *listen*.

Active learners work through this set of mental gymnastics every day. They work on their humility and maintaining an open mind (more on this in part two) because they see the value truth-tellers bring. Over the years, the truth-tellers on the teams I led made all the difference. Sometimes I wanted to kick them out of my office, but I always listened.

At Yum!, Jonathan Blum, who was in charge of public affairs, was one of my truth-tellers. He would come into my office and tell me that I had alienated somebody in a meeting, that an idea I had wasn't very good, or that somebody on the team had to go. I would feel like throwing him out, and he could tell. But he just let my irritation slide off him and kept reiterating the truth until I listened. And I listened because I knew he had my best interests at heart. We all need truth-tellers like that.

Active learners don't just wait for truth-tellers to show up, though. We seek them out. We embrace them. We keep them close rather than shut them out. And we ask them for the truth.

When I asked Chris Kempczinski, the CEO of McDonald's, what one piece of advice he would give to aspiring leaders, he came back fast with: "Find somebody who's going to tell you the truth. Because as you . . . get into bigger and bigger jobs, there are fewer and fewer people who are willing to tell you the truth. And if people are *not* going to tell you the truth, you're going to miss stuff and you're not going to be as successful."

The biggest truth-teller in my life is my wife, Wendy. Along with my parents, she is the biggest contributor to my success. And sometimes she pisses me off. Sometimes I disagree with her. Still, I try to listen—because she's often right. And I *ask* for her opinion constantly. Every time I give a speech, she gives me a letter grade. "That was a B," she'll say, which immediately cues my ego to send up a defense. "A B! Five other people just told me it was great!" She'll just repeat the truth, "Well, it was a B." So I take a deep breath and ask, "*Why* was it a B?" She'll tell me that the opening wasn't great, or a joke didn't land, or whatever it was that kept me from getting an A.

I've worked on being coachable, and I've learned so much from her about how to improve my speeches, podcasts, and books. But here's the other big benefit of truth-tellers: when they tell you you've done well, you can believe them absolutely. When I get an A from Wendy, I know without a doubt I'm doing my best work.

Tyler Toney and Coby Cotton, founding members of the five-person Dude Perfect team, the trick-shot YouTube stars and sports entertainers, told me that truth-telling is how they get to their best ideas. They started working together in college, and they're all hyper-competitive. "You've got to have thick skin around here," Ty said, "because you'll get told, 'That idea is terrible.'" Coby agreed: "The judgment comes quick and hard. But as long as you're willing to keep throwing out ideas . . . "

They've found that good ideas are often sparked by terrible ideas. "Your idea was terrible, Coby," Coby said, mimicking what he's heard from the other guys, "But fortunately, we pulled *one* piece of gold out of it." Their creative process would never work, they would never get to the A ideas, if they couldn't handle the truth. And obviously, they do get to the As, given that they have nearly *60 million followers* and more than *15 billion views* on YouTube, host a *Thursday Night Football* show for the NFL, and field new opportunities every day.

I can't believe I'm quoting a notorious gangster and liar in a chapter on truth-telling, but John Gotti gave the world some good advice when he said, "You only lie when you're afraid." If people are afraid to tell us the truth, because of our reaction or the possible negative consequences, we won't have many truth-tellers in our lives. If they tell us the truth and we don't take action, don't hold ourselves accountable to the truth, they'll stop sharing it with us. What's the point, if nothing changes, if we learn nothing?

If you think you might be at risk of shutting out or shutting down the truth-tellers in your life, use Alexa von Tobel's guidance: "It's not about being right. *It's about getting to the right answer.*" As the founder and CEO of LearnVest and the founder and managing partner of Inspired Capital, she's at least partially responsible for investing hundreds of millions of dollars and the success or demise of companies in its funds. She places high value on people who will consistently and passionately tell her that she's wrong, who will say, "That was dumb. Don't do that." She's a believer in the idea that Adam Grant shared succinctly in his newsletter: **"Intellectual friction isn't a relationship bug. It's a feature of learning."**[3]

"I enjoy going out of my way to create psychological safety so people can tell me things that I have to hear to get to the right answer," Alexa told me. She also shared with me a story from her friend Mark Kelly, Arizona senator and husband of former congresswoman Gabby Giffords, who in 2011, was shot during a public event. When Mark was in a room with a team of doctors trying to understand the surgical options for Gabby, "he put the doctors in order of seniority, made the youngest go first, and then went backwards." He didn't want the answers, the possibilities, or the truth to be swayed by politics or hierarchy. Alexa keeps that story in mind whenever she's trying to get to the right answer with a group.

Active learners understand something essential: **the more you tell the truth, the more you'll hear the truth.** So they become truth-tellers themselves. To be a good truth-teller is an art, though. It begins with showing that you have the person's best interests in mind. It requires some optimism about their ability to achieve something better and a willingness to help them along the way. Making this effort puts the listener in acceptance mode and helps bypass the immediate defenses of the brain so that they can see possibilities.

Seek out the truth, ask for it, make it safe for people to say it, and tell it. When you do, you'll learn and grow in all the best ways, and so will those around you.

Learning from Your Truth-Tellers

- Do you have truth-tellers in your life, or enough of them?

- What important question could you ask a truth-teller that might change your perspective on a goal, a plan, a relationship?

- Have you been told a truth that you haven't acted on?
  What could you do to show you're listening?

Chapter 5

Viral Videos, Syringes, and Rats

The last thing I ever wanted to be is a CSE—a crisis survival expert. But I am one, and I earned the title the hard way. If I shared every crisis I've faced and what I learned from it here, there wouldn't be room in the book for anything else.

Crises are a fact of leadership and life. They show up just when we think we've hit smooth sailing or when we think we can't possibly handle one more thing. Still, active learners use them to improve, no matter the context. In fact, **I'd argue there's more to mine in a crisis or failure than in a success** (although there's plenty to learn from winning, too, which is why I wrote the next chapter). Some of my most powerful insights have come during the darkest moments. When a new crisis shows up, I put my active learning into high gear and absorb everything I can.

Each crisis can teach us something unique, but all crises instill a few universal lessons, if we let them. First, they teach us that we're nearly always *capable* of making it through. Second, they teach us how to *avoid* similar crises in the future. And third, they teach us *how to survive* and even come out stronger and better on the other side, so we're more prepared for the next new and different crisis.

Around the time that I was preparing to leave Yum! in 2016, I was dealing with a high volume of change in my life and work: I was shaping my departure with the board; we were spinning off Yum! China as a separate publicly traded company; my wife, Wendy, was struggling with issues related to her type 1 diabetes (one of the main reasons I was leaving); and I was working on ideas for what I would do next.

At the time, an old friend, Jamie Coulter, who had been a major Pizza Hut franchisee and then founded Lone Star Steakhouse, asked if I would be interested in helping another restaurant company go public. I thanked him for thinking of me but told him I was ready to move on from the restaurant business. "What else have you been up to?" I asked.

"Well, you're never going to believe it, but I just made it through stage four breast cancer. I had a double mastectomy not long ago."

I went home and told Wendy his startling news. I didn't even realize men could get breast cancer, but Jamie had told me that the numbers are probably much higher than we realize.

A couple of months later, I noticed a little bump that felt like a pebble on my left pec when I was working out. My doctor told me that it was just a cyst (I had had others) and not to worry about it unless it got bigger. It kept nagging at me, though, so when I got back from a trip to China, I decided to get another opinion from a cancer surgeon. One look and he told me, "This isn't breast cancer. Men who get breast cancer are almost always overweight and have other risk factors. You don't have anything to be concerned about."

"That may be true, but I'm still worried," I said. "Is there anything I can do to get it checked out."

Reluctantly, he sent me off for a mammogram—which led to an ultrasound, which led to a radiologist recommending a biopsy. "Let's do it right now," I said. I wanted an answer. They would have the results in twenty-four hours.

The next day I received a wonderful letter congratulating me on my career success and what I had accomplished at Yum!—from Jamie

Coulter (who sadly passed away while I was working on this manuscript). I'm usually an optimistic person, but I saw it as a sign.

And I was right. I had breast cancer.

I believe I had an advantage going into cancer treatment—a CSE advantage. Beyond my own experience with crises, I'd learned about managing them from some great teachers and teachable moments. Craig Weatherup was president of Pepsi-Cola when I was a COO. In 1993, someone placed syringes in Pepsi cans. It was national news. Craig handled everything in a manner that only earned Pepsi more brand loyalty. I'll never forget walking into his office just before he was getting ready to go on national TV. "Craig, what do you do before you go on the Larry King show to talk about something like this?"

He looked at me calmly and said, "I read my mail."

In crises, I've learned to start with Craig's advice and move forward with a straightforward plan:

- Don't panic.

- Get the facts and deal in reality.

- Make good decisions based on those facts.

- Focus on what you can control, not what you can't.

And that's what I did with my cancer diagnosis. I started by not panicking and knowing that we can handle more than we think. I turned to the most reputable experts. I got multiple opinions. I chose my doctors based on who I thought would help me achieve my goals. I studied what others had done to improve their odds. I learned that Lance Armstrong (who, despite his other failings, had a lot to teach about surviving cancer) worked out twice a day throughout his treatment, even during chemo and radiation, so that's what I did. I especially focused on the most important thing within my control, which was my attitude, and I believe that is a big factor in why I am still here, cancer-free, years later.

This isn't a book on recovering from trauma, and I'm not a psychologist. But anytime you're talking about crisis and resilience, it's helpful to remember Martin Seligman's three Ps of "learned helplessness"—personalization, permanence, and pervasiveness.

Let's say you lose your job because your company fell on hard times. Personalization might make you say, "If I had worked harder, they wouldn't have laid me off." Permanence might make you think, "I'm never going to find another job that I'll like as much as that one." And pervasiveness might make you believe, "I'll probably lose my partner next. Why would they stay with an unemployed loser?"

As Sheryl Sandberg and Adam Grant wrote in *Option B*, on her recovery from the early and tragic death of her husband, "The three P's play like the flip side of the pop song 'Everything Is Awesome'—'everything is awful.' The loop in your head repeats, 'It's my fault this is awful. My whole life is awful. And it's always going to be awful.'"[1]

When we're in this place mentally, what are our chances of learning? And what are the chances of coming through it whole—or even better than we were before? **We can only learn and then do something with what we learn when we have some optimism about the future and a belief in our ability to influence it.** So I did what I needed to do to stay clear and positive and to maintain my hope and faith.

This ability had served me well in good times and in bad. Years before my cancer diagnosis, when I was just weeks into my job as CEO of Yum!, our *only* food distributor, AmeriServe, declared bankruptcy. We had heard rumors it wasn't paying suppliers, and that was a problem, considering it was responsible for getting food from those suppliers to our thousands of restaurants. The AmeriServe leaders assured us they weren't going to declare bankruptcy—and kept assuring us until just hours before they declared bankruptcy.

All along, my team suspected they would, but when they made the announcement, our stock plummeted, and we were backed into a corner. We either loaned AmeriServe money to continue operating and preserve our relationships with suppliers or we let our restaurants go dark.

That event yielded two blunt-edged reminders: First, lean on others, especially experts who know more than you. At Yum! that was our CFO Dave Deno, our legal counsel Chris Campbell, and our COO Aylwin Lewis. They negotiated this big, complex financial crisis and made sure it didn't consume the energy and attention of the entire company.

Second, I was reminded that when you are the source of a crisis, you have to be honest and transparent (AmeriServe was not) by following these three steps:

1. Be truthful and get the word out. People will forgive you if you tell them the truth and keep them informed.

2. Explain specifically how you're handling the situation right now.

3. Lay out what you're going to do to make sure it doesn't happen again.

Taking these three steps is a forcing function for active learning. If you're going to tell the truth, you must first learn the truth. If you're going to explain how you're handling the situation, you must learn the best way to handle the situation. If you're going to lay out a better process for the future, you must learn enough to create and deploy that better process. And it may not be explicitly stated in this list, but what should be clear is that **you can't try to spin your way out, to blame and point fingers, and hope to learn anything of value.**

That was a hard lesson that Oscar Munoz, CEO of United Airlines, had to learn in 2017, when a sixty-nine-year-old passenger, Dr. David Dao, was dragged off flight 3411 from Louisville to Chicago. When I asked him about the mistakes that followed, he said, "It was maybe my biggest *sort* of mistake *ever.*"

Four United employees needed to get to Louisville to staff a flight the next day. In these situations, they're considered "must-ride" passengers. The flight was sold out, so the supervisor asked for volunteers to get off the plane, offering the usual perks. No volunteers came forward, so they chose four passengers at random and then made the announcement that they needed to leave the plane. Dr. Dao was chosen. He immediately called United Airlines and explained that he had to get home to see patients the next day. United didn't acquiesce. When he refused to deplane, a United employee called security. When he still refused, they manhandled him, he screamed, and as they dragged him from his seat down the aisle, he hit his head. The scene was recorded and uploaded to Twitter (now X). The videos, which are awful to watch, went viral. One was viewed almost 7 million times in a day. One hit Weibo, a Chinese microblogging site, and 480 million people watched it (it was originally thought that Dr. Dao is Chinese American, but he is Vietnamese American).

"We [United] may have been the first global corporation to get hit by this viral sort of Twitter backlash," Oscar said to me. (I knew a little of what they experienced. In 2007, a video of rats getting into a KFC after closing hours in New York City hit YouTube and tanked our sales.) The backlash for United seemed justified. Even President Donald Trump called the handling of the situation terrible.

How United responded made the situation even worse. First, it tried to explain it away and deflect. It pointed out that it was aviation security that removed Dr. Dao, not United employees. But as Oscar said later, that context is irrelevant when somebody has been assaulted. United even seemed to blame the incident on Dr. Dao's behavior.

In an initial statement, the company said that the flight had been *overbooked*, which is a regulatory term and issue. So, it started using the term *re-accommodated*. "When a human has been dragged and beaten off an aircraft, the word *re-accommodated* is an awful, awful choice of words, I am sure you'll agree—as did the rest of the world," Oscar said. And it was made worse because it did issue an initial apology, but only for "re-accommodating" passengers.

It was time for Oscar to step into the spotlight and go on national TV to address the situation before it spiraled further. The coaching he got was to continue to deflect. He told me, "Somewhere in the middle of the night, I literally got out of bed and fell to my knees, not being a pious person necessarily, but kind of looking above for some level of direction. And I remembered . . . my maternal grandmother, who I grew up with. She was an incredible human who never complained, never blamed anyone." He felt a calm come over him. He still wasn't sure what he was going to say on TV the next morning, but he knew what he needed to do.

In the interview with ABC's *Good Morning America,* he said he was ashamed. He apologized to Dr. Dao and his family and the rest of the people on the flight. He said that it would never happen again, and then explained what United would do to make sure it didn't. And he made it clear that Dr. Dao was not at fault. The funny thing, Oscar shared, was the audible gasps he heard from the producers and his own people as he talked. He wasn't saying what his people thought he was *supposed* to say or what the producers *expected* him to say. But he knew he didn't want to spend years recanting a blame story.

United followed through and put new systems in place to make things better for passengers. "My barometer is the business schools around the country that initially wrote it as a case of exactly what not to do," Oscar told me. Those business cases shifted to become lessons in "It's never too late to do the right thing."

Active learners try to do the right thing in a crisis because it helps them spot opportunity for growth and improvement and more learning. For example, we came out of the KFC rat crisis with infinitely superior pest control processes. Behind every calamity—the big ones and the small ones—lies an opportunity to protect yourself from the same kind of problem in the future, build stronger relationships, rewrite the rules when the world has shifted on you, or discover an idea that will lead to greater success. It's also an opportunity to decide what you stand for and what you value and let that guide you.

One powerful crisis story comes from Niren Chaudhary, CEO of Panera Bread and a former colleague at Yum! A year into his tenure with Panera, with promising growth ahead, Covid-19 hit. Panera's sales dropped by 50 percent almost overnight. Niren didn't panic. Instead, he worked with his leadership team to find ways to become part of the solution. They set up curbside pickup across a thousand cafés within a week. In one more week, they thought up, developed, and executed an online grocery delivery service, getting essential items, baked goods, dairy products, and fresh produce to customers who were stuck at home or afraid to go to grocery stores.

Like me, Niren went into the crisis with a CSE advantage—and also one he never wanted. He had learned the power of being part of the solution from his daughter Aisha, an amazing role model. Aisha was born with severe combined immunodeficiency, the same illness that her older sister had died of at seven months old. Aisha made it through the early years with a bone marrow transplant and chemotherapy but developed pulmonary fibrosis that took her life at eighteen. Before she passed, she spent much of her time sharing her story, speaking at conferences, and writing a book to help others going through similar traumatic experiences. (You can learn more about her life, story, and influence in the Netflix documentary *Black Sunshine Baby*.) She found purpose and resilience by focusing on how she could be part of the solution. And that's how Niren handled the crisis in front of him.

. . .

We can all relate to Henry Kissinger's famous line, "There cannot be a crisis next week. My schedule is already full."[2] It would be great if we could just schedule crises for when we think we'll have the knowledge, energy, or time to deal with them, but they are fickle things. Another crisis, big or small, is coming on its own terms. Active learners pause, take stock, and try to process every insight from the calamities they're already experiencing. They figure out how to use the insights to build confidence and resilience, hope and optimism.

If you look back over your life, you'll find moments when you've done exactly that. Along the way, you learned things about yourself and about the world and about how to succeed despite the circumstances. Put that CSE advantage to use when the next crisis arises—hopefully not next week, when I'm sure your schedule is already full.

Learning from Crises

Think about a crisis you've dealt with in the past year.

- What did you do that had the biggest positive impact?

- What did you do that didn't turn out well?

- What could you do tomorrow to help avoid a similar problem in the future? Or what will you do differently the next time a similar crisis arises?

Chapter 6

Follow the Bright Spots

Learn from winning

In 2022, Yum! Brands marked its twenty-fifth anniversary with a leadership meeting and celebration. The leadership team asked me, as cofounder, to speak. When I thought about what I would say, I went back to the very beginning.

By 1997, the restaurant division at PepsiCo had failed to meet expectations for five years, and Wall Street wanted the company to jettison it. So PepsiCo did, by spinning it out into its own company; that's how I became cofounder of Yum! Some doubted Yum! could stand on its own. It didn't help that we started off with a tense relationship with our franchisees, nearly $5 billion in debt, and a junk bond balance sheet.

The doubts were unfounded. When I left two decades later, in 2016, Yum! had doubled its number of restaurants to more than forty thousand. The stock price was ten times higher than when we started. And our business in China had become so strong that we spun it off as its own public company.

I thought my speech should focus on how we managed to do that. For me, the answer was straightforward: we learned from winning and by recognizing the people who made it happen.

Even in our tough state at the start, I knew we had everything we needed to build a dynasty that would stand the test of time: great market share, leadership talent, a strong global presence. But none of that would matter if we couldn't produce results. PepsiCo had wanted to jettison the restaurants specifically because they hadn't produced results. They had failed to meet expectations for five years. John Weinberg, a member of our board and the legendary vice chairman of Goldman Sachs, cemented that idea for me. The great companies get great results year after year after year, he told me. Deliver consistent growth and your stock will go through the roof. That sparked an idea. We needed to learn from those great, dynastic companies and from our own *consistently* high-performing restaurants.

I took the Partners' Council—the presidents and chief operating officers of each division of our company as well as my direct reports, fourteen people in all—on tours of dynastic companies, including General Electric (a rocket ship at the time), Walmart, Home Depot, Southwest Airlines, and Target. By getting the partners involved, I knew we'd all own the ideas generated along the way. I also knew that more people looking for ways to win meant we'd find the *best* ideas.

Best-practice visits are common and sometimes can feel like meaningless field trips, but for us, they were inspiring. We witnessed other leaders in action. Ken Langone, a cofounder of Home Depot and the investment banker who took the company public, was out in a store parking lot rounding up shopping carts and returning them to the front of the store when we met him, because that's what Home Depot wants every associate to do, no matter how high up. As we entered the store with him, an associate with a developmental disability ran up to Ken and asked if he could show him something he'd done that he was proud of. Ken left us standing there for ten minutes to be with the associate. Here we learned that winning meant small actions that would signal to an entire organization that the way you take care of business is by taking care of your people.

After the best-practices tour, the Partners' Council retreated to the Adirondacks to share what we had learned and apply it to our company. When we broke it down, we realized that we all admired the same five essential things about those companies, which we called the Yum! Dynasty Drivers:

- A focus on a culture where everyone counts

- Customer and sales mania

- Competitive differentiation

- Continuity in people and processes

- Consistent year-over-year results

Next, we looked internally at the best-performing restaurants to see what they had in common. The result of all this learning-from-winning effort was our How We Work Together principles, which we would later evolve into How We *Win* Together:

- *Customer focus.* In successful restaurants, team members always listen and respond to their customers.

- *Belief in people.* We want all our team members to understand that their contribution is valued.

- *Recognition.* We want to reward and recognize those contributions every chance we get and have fun doing it.

- *Coaching and support.* All leaders need to be more than just bosses; they need to be invested in the success of those they lead.

- *Accountability.* Because results matter.

- *Excellence.* All success comes from taking pride in doing a great job.

- *Positive energy.* You can feel it when you walk into a place where customers are having a good time and the team is doing a great job.

- *Teamwork.* Because we make it happen together.

I believe this focus on winning and the mindset of *learning from wins* was one of the biggest factors in our sustained success. We celebrated wins more than we punished losses. We spread winning ideas. We assessed how our competitors were winning. We kept at it month-by-month, year-by-year. John Weinberg had told me to shoot for 10 percent growth in our earnings per share every year—we delivered *13 percent for thirteen straight years*. And the year it turned twenty-five, Yum! broke its own *and* the industry record for new store openings.

Active learners follow this pattern every day. **They learn as much as they can from others' wins—from people and teams that know something they might not. And they don't miss any opportunity to learn from their own wins**.

Studying winners gives you know-how that can make all the difference. Ask a hundred people who read business books for their favorite title; I bet seventy will choose *Good to Great* by Jim Collins. Why? Because it's highly distilled active learning. Jim studied winners and then distilled what he learned about how they won into actionable insights. (In the next chapter, we'll talk about learning from losing, also important, and the source of Jim's subsequent book, *How the Mighty Fall*.)

Surprisingly, some people don't make the effort to study winners. Maybe that's because it means admitting that others are winning more than they are. They might have to face up to the reality that they don't have all the answers. Active learners fight that kind of thinking because they know it only leads to mediocrity.

For example, early in my time as CEO at Yum!, I took a hard look at our same-store sales—growing at a decent 2 to 3 percent clip. But McDonald's was running at 5 to 7 percent. We were doing well, but McDonald's was *winning*. I knew we could do better, but knowing *how* we could do better meant *learning how* McDonald's was winning. Could we find key ideas or strategies in its success? We initiated a global McDonald's immersion day for all senior teams *around the world*. Every team spent a full day visiting McDonald's stores to observe, analyze, and gather ideas. We let teams draw their own conclusions about how McDonald's was winning.

Each team shared observations and ideas, and from this mass of insights, we learned most of what we needed to improve. McDonald's served a huge number of customers breakfast before our teams were out of bed, and many stores stayed open round the clock. It sold coffee all day, and that was a great value play (it doesn't take much money to produce a cup of coffee). It also offered a $0.99 value menu that drove customer volume. And it did a decent dessert business.

Coffee and dessert were virtually nonexistent at Yum! restaurants, breakfast was rare, and nearly everything we served cost more than $1. So we went to work attacking these weak spots and implementing a sales layers strategy. We rolled out ideas like the KFC Snacker, a simple, affordable chicken sandwich that was an instant smash. We stayed open later, came up with Taco Bell's innovative fourth meal for late night business, and launched Taco Bell's great breakfast menu. The result was substantially better growth over time.

And we used that success to learn even more. As much as we can learn from other winners, learning from our own wins can be even more powerful. I wrote in the last chapter that I've learned more from the tough times than I have from the good, and that's true, but just *barely*. The challenge is that it can seem *easier* to learn from losses. The lessons are more obvious. It can take more effort and focus to learn from wins, because when we're winning, it's easy to assume that we'll keep on winning. It's easy to achieve a big goal, think "Nailed it!" and then move on to the next one.

In *Switch*, psychologist Chip Heath explained that we're far more likely to focus our analysis on problems and failures than on successes. But some of the biggest and best changes come when we find a *bright spot*, a success that seems out of the ordinary, and try to understand it. Following the bright spots to a win is a lot more motivating than slogging through problem after problem. And the bright spots often show us more about how to solve the problems holding us back, anyway.

Active learners don't walk away from a win without a backward glance. They analyze and assess. What made the difference? What hurdles did they have to overcome along the way and how did they? What did they learn about themselves or the people around them? What they're looking for are bright spots—insights into process, discipline, and revelations from innovative moments they can leverage. They use what they discover to make the next win a bit easier, more likely, or bigger. And they do this consistently. The great Vince Lombardi put it plainly: "Winning is a habit."

One of the best things you can learn from your own wins is not all that different from what you learn from crises: that you *can* make it. Tom Brady told me during our podcast, "I'm never going to be in a game for the rest of my career where I don't think we can win. It's not a false confidence. It's a real confidence." He was describing what he learned from the experience of leading the Patriots to the largest comeback in Super Bowl history against the Atlanta Falcons. At almost halfway through the third quarter, the Patriots were down 28 to 3.

When Dr. John Noseworthy became the CEO of the Mayo Clinic, the Great Recession and lower reimbursements were putting the health-care system in the red. "To be honest," he told me, "the margins were too thin for us to continue to invest in research and education."

The solution he saw was to restructure so that Mayo Clinic could operate more efficiently, while also helping doctors better understand the business of medicine, especially how their decisions impact the bottom line.

It was not a popular idea, especially with the long-tenured doctors and leaders of the organization who were worried about the culture of care and the focus on patients. In one meeting, a friend and fifteen-year colleague of John's stood up and said, "You're going to ruin the Mayo Clinic."

But he was confident that he could help doctors make better choices about where to spend money to deliver the highest-quality care. And he believed it *because it had been done before*. Mayo Clinic had faced tough times in the past and had won by doing exactly what he was proposing. And that's what he said when he was accused of ruining the organization. "I said, 'No, I'm not actually.' We did this during the Depression. And it worked. We did it during World War II. And it worked. And we're gonna do it now. And it'll work. And it did." Mayo Clinic kept its doors open during a tough financial period, but more than that, it increased the quality of care delivered.

When you're in a tough situation or slogging your way to a goal, it can be hard to stay motivated and inspired. It can be hard to keep an open mind. Fear can overwhelm you. Some say fear of failure is what drives champions. I don't think that's nearly enough. You need to chase the joy of winning, too. The book *Fearless Golf* by Gio Valiante perfectly sums up what I've experienced: when you let fear of failure take the reins, you usually start losing. Operating from a position of fear and ego limits you. It narrows your thinking. It makes you less able to learn, grow, and improve. Once you focus on losing, or how you could lose, you do lose. But if you build your belief in your ability to win and if you're focused on what you can do now to win, you're operating from a place of mastery. You're opening yourself up to what's possible, what you can learn, and what you can leverage.

Not long before I read *Fearless Golf*, I had reached a major goal on a very challenging golf course: I shot my age, sixty-eight, four under par. I was elated and spread the word quickly and to as many friends as I could—and then I hit the worst slump I've ever had. After reading the book, I recognized that I was playing ego-driven, fear-based golf. I was worried what people would think if I couldn't keep playing that well, or if I lost to somebody who wasn't as strong a player or who was five years older. It took reconnecting with the joy of winning and my love of the game to move past it and refocus on mastery, or how I could keep improving with every shot. And a year later, I shot my age again, sixty-nine.

When you take the time to reflect on how far you've come and the series of wins it took to get you here, you're reminded that you're capable, that you can trust your instincts and what you or your team learned from past experiences. And if you just keep moving, you'll learn something soon that could make all the difference.

When we win, we learn the joy of it, the exhilaration, especially if we stop and celebrate and revel in those feelings. It's that joy of winning that will inspire us for the next adventure and open us up to all the lessons it has to offer.

Learning from Winning

- Who are the people or organizations accomplishing the things you'd like to accomplish? Have you deeply analyzed how they're doing it?

- Pick a big win of your own from the last few years and answer this question: What specifically made the difference in your success?

- Create a list of greatest hits or a highlight reel of your most inspiring wins. When you need to relearn what's possible, or when you need a boost of confidence or motivation, pull it out.

Chapter 7

The Worst Way to Get on SNL

I was forty years old and serving as chief marketing officer for Pepsi-Co's beverage division and something big was happening: colas were losing ground to what we called "alternative beverages." Drinks like Snapple and flavored waters were hot, partially because of the focus on healthier living. Clear beverages were the hottest of the hot new market segment. Clear *everything* was popular then; marketers even refer to the era as the "Clear Craze."

Clear was winning, so I thought, "Why can't we do a clear Pepsi?" (I'm a big believer in pattern thinking, which you'll read more about in part two. It doesn't always produce genius.)

I thought clear Pepsi—we would call it Crystal Pepsi—was the biggest idea I'd ever had. I thought it would be my career maker. Early indications did nothing to tamp my enthusiasm. Focus groups loved it. It was a novel idea from one of the most recognizable brands in the world. The first day Crystal Pepsi came off the line to supply our test market in Colorado, it led the *CBS Evening News* with Dan Rather. People started sending cases of Crystal Pepsi to parts of the country where it wasn't available yet, like they did in the early days of Coors beer. This was a big deal. It was becoming a cultural phenomenon, and I thought I was the genius who had just created a breakout product. I envisioned record sales and profits for Pepsi-Cola. I was a clear-crazed evangelist ready to take it national.

But as the great Paul Harvey would say, "And now . . . for the rest of the story."

My first clue that there might be a problem came even before the test market release, while I was still blinded by enthusiasm. I needed permission from Don Kendall, the founder of PepsiCo, to launch a new product with the Pepsi name. Don was a straight-talking mountain of a man. When I explained the idea, he just said, "I don't like it, but if you do . . ."

Next came unwanted feedback from the board members of the Pepsi-Cola Bottling Association. They told me it was a good idea with a key weakness: it didn't taste enough like Pepsi. I said, "Well, it's not supposed to taste exactly like Pepsi because it's supposed to be a lighter cola with a lighter taste."

"Yeah," they said, "but you're *calling* it Pepsi." I rebutted with more facts from our market research and then plowed ahead, pushing to get it to market in time for a big Super Bowl ad campaign. By the way, adding time pressure to a potential failure in the making often seems to cement the outcome.

The doubters were right. For all the initial hype, Crystal Pepsi failed as soon as the novelty faded. It *didn't* taste enough like Pepsi. And rushing it to national distribution created quality issues.

We got slaughtered. *Saturday Night Live* lampooned us in a skit called "Crystal Gravy."

I felt like the question, "Remember Crystal Pepsi?" became a one-line cautionary tale. And more than a decade after we pulled Crystal Pepsi from the market, *Time* magazine put it on its list of "The 100 Worst Ideas of the Century," alongside hydrogen-filled blimps, psychic hotlines, and spray-on hair.

That was a rough time. I remember walking down the hall thinking that people were wondering why I still had my job or whispering that I wouldn't have it for long. But through it all, I learned two lasting lessons. The first was that when people **with experience share**

their opinions with you, listen. I was so convinced I had come up with the next big Pepsi product that I didn't listen to anyone who was telling me to slow down and assess. I wasn't learning as I should have been. To this day I regret that I didn't listen, because if I had, I think we could have gotten through the core issues and Crystal Pepsi could have worked. (More on listening in part two.)

The second lesson: work for people and organizations that understand **you can't grow and innovate if you don't take risks and sometimes fail.** That's the mindset (and culture) of active learners. Pepsi values innovation and knows that sometimes risks don't pay off. I never truly felt like my job was on the line because my risky idea hadn't worked out. (It also helped that the bottlers sold Crystal Pepsi with premium pricing, because *they* knew that once the novelty wore off, people wouldn't come back. In the end, they made money, and the brief popularity of Crystal Pepsi helped Pepsi-Cola meet its goals for the year.)

Unfortunately, fear of failure can keep us from taking risks that lead to great learning opportunities. If that feels familiar, let me remind you that many things that don't go to plan turn out better than you can imagine. And even when they don't, what you learn along the way is much greater than if things had turned out just right.

Carol Dweck, one of the greatest authorities on what it takes to stay open to learning and develop a growth mindset, didn't start out believing that failure could be a good thing. "You were smart, or you weren't," she wrote in the bestseller *Mindset*, "and failure meant you weren't. It was that simple. If you could arrange successes and avoid failures (at all costs), you could stay smart."[1] But she also wanted to understand how people cope when they *do* fail. So, in her research, she would give kids easy puzzles and hard puzzles and study how they responded. The big surprise, the turning moment in her life and career, was realizing how much kids relished those hard puzzles, how they kept trying, and what they said about the experience. The kids not only weren't discouraged by failure, "they didn't even think they were failing. *They thought they were learning.*" This book you're reading right now is about flipping everything we experience, think, and do to make it about learning, and these young kids had it all figured out.

To learn from failures, we must be willing to fail in the first place. We must battle our fear, take the risk, see what happens, and then assess with a laser eye on opportunities for growth and improvement. Shantanu Narayen, the CEO of Adobe Systems, is a firm believer in this principle. Many CEOs would want to come on a podcast to talk exclusively about their successes, but he didn't hesitate to share his failed product ideas and even an early business he had started that didn't pan out. "Let's also celebrate products that were perhaps not commercial successes," he told me, "that may have been commercial failures, but the learnings from them were really what enabled us to build another product. . . . Celebrate people who tried something, took the initiative." He doesn't even like using the word *failure* because he is so focused on the learning experience instead.

That's the essence of learning from failure: you can't change the past, so you shouldn't beat yourself up about it. But you can change how you move forward from there.

It starts with a growth mindset, because if we see our missteps as signs that *we* are failures, why would we want to admit our role in them? Active learners aren't afraid to hold themselves accountable, because they know it leads to growth. Larry Senn, the corporate culture guru who helped me develop and roll out the culture at Yum!, tackles this with an accountability exercise.

Start by thinking about a situation that's going poorly and name all the ways in which you're getting screwed over. Then, break away from that thinking and instead take total responsibility for your role. Ask, "What could I have done differently that might have resulted in a different outcome?"

For example, roughly 50 percent of small retail startups fail, and about 80 percent of boutique clothing stores fail. So how has boutique jeweler Kendra Scott been so successful? By examining how and why her first boutique failed. She launched the Hat Box at nineteen years old, selling hats for men and women, but the hat craze she was hoping for never emerged. After five years, she was out of business, burned out, and broke. What's more, her stepfather tragically passed away from brain cancer at about the same time, and Kendra told me that she felt as though she had let him and her whole family down. She felt like a complete failure.

At the hat store, she had also sold jewelry she designed and made herself. She would fill up a few shelves, and within a day, it would all be gone, but she didn't pick up on this success. She was so blinded by the hat idea, her version of Crystal Pepsi, that she didn't see the potential in her jewelry—at first. But when she couldn't focus on hats anymore and realized that she was *still* getting calls about the jewelry, she finally recognized that maybe this jewelry thing had legs. Today, that jewelry thing is worth well more than a billion dollars.

The failure propelled the success. By finally treating it as something to mine rather than be paralyzed by it, she learned the ways in which retail fails and how to avoid them. She learned to pay attention to the signs of opportunity rather than blindly follow an idea to its death.

In her great book *Be Bad First*, Erika Andersen writes about the idea of mastery, something active learners work hard at pursuing. Acquiring skills and knowledge faster demands that we develop "that ability to accept the discomfort and disequilibrium that is an inevitable part of learning something new. Sometimes that involves accepting failure, but more often it simply means learning to be okay with slowness, awkwardness, not being clear about things, having to ask embarrassing questions—that is, learning to be okay with being bad first on the way to getting good."[2]

Olympic gold medalist in skating Scott Hamilton told me a story about his son's ice hockey team getting slaughtered in a game. His son came off the ice upset and angry.

Scott said, "Let's break it down. What happened today?"

"Well," his son said, "they just skate faster than me."

"And that means what?"

"I've got to work harder on my skating."

"OK, good. What else?"

"They took the puck every time I had it."

"What did you learn from that?"

"I've got to work on my stick handling."

Then his son said, "I just don't like losing."

"OK, let's say you won today. What would you have learned?"

A pause and then his son said, "Nothing."

Well, as we've seen, you *can* learn from winning, but I understand the point Scott was making. "I'm a big fan of failure," he told me. "**Failure is 100 percent information, only information.** If we can break it down to information—instead of this horrible, toxic, scarring, disfiguring identity that we must carry around with us for the rest of our life— we can move forward toward excellence or toward the best version of ourselves. . . . I've fallen on the ice a minimum of 41,600 times. But it's getting up 41,600 times that allows you to understand the process of learning, the process of growing, and the process of getting to where you want to be."

I'm happy to say that I've been able to get up after a fall many times. But I'm sorry to say that it took me too long to understand why I kept falling and specifically my pattern of conviction in the rightness of my ideas. I never really escaped until I did another simple exercise with Larry Senn. He shared the quote below and asked the leaders in the room to count the Fs:

THE MOST EFFECTIVE OF ALL HUMAN FEARS WHICH PREVENT THE DEVELOPMENT OF FULL POTEN-TIAL ARE THE FEAR OF FAILURE AND THE FEAR OF SUCCESS. . . . IT IS A THIEF OF INNOVATION AND OF SATISFACTION.

At first, I counted nine Fs, which I can tell you is the wrong answer.* Being wrong wasn't nearly as revealing to me, though, as the fact that I was totally convinced that I was right. Larry asked me how much I would bet on it, and I said, "The ranch."

My combination of passion and competitiveness means I can become so attached to my point of view that I fail to consider any others. This isn't something you correct once and move on. Active learners aren't perfect. They're human beings who have to work at their learning behaviors. Years after Crystal Pepsi, I *still* managed to fall prey to the same mistake again when I decided it was time for me to move on from Yum! In 2016, I identified Greg Creed as the best successor for CEO. I decided that I would assume the role of executive chairman, like many other founders had—Sam Walton of Walmart, Fred Smith of FedEx to name two. I imagined playing the kind of adviser-partner role that Andy Pearson had played for me when he became chairman of Yum! and I became president. Together, we could guide the company through the transition, and eventually we would phase out my involvement.

I had written a book called *Taking People with You*, but somehow, in this instance, I didn't do that. I just told the board members my plan. I didn't have a meeting with them to explain my thinking, to detail the kind of role I would play, to reassure them that I didn't want to undercut Greg, or to explain the kind of timeline I thought was realistic. I didn't do any of that. I just assumed they'd be onboard and aligned and would let me figure it out. After all, in my view, I had helped build this great company, and everybody should have recognized that I *obviously* still had the company's best interests at heart. The dramatic success I had had gave me a sense of entitlement that I've never liked in others. I didn't put myself in the shoes of all the board members.

---

* The correct answer is 15. The reason I missed so many Fs is that, like most people, I overlooked the F in every "of" because they have a V sound and come at the end of the smallest words.

Changing a CEO is one of the most important decisions a board can make, and it needs careful management, no matter how well the company is doing or how much success the outgoing CEO had.

In our first meeting about the transition, it was clear that a few of the board members thought I should leave right away, partially because that's what they had done in their CEO roles. From there, it went downhill. I felt betrayed by some people because of how they maneuvered around me. In the end, I served in the executive chairman role only briefly, and my time in it wasn't what I had hoped. It was not how I wanted to end my time with a company I had founded and devoted most of my career to building.

Now, years later, I can look back and say that the board handled some things poorly, but I was just as responsible for the breakdowns, maybe more so.

Nothing about that experience changed how I felt about Yum!, the people I worked with, including the board members, or what I accomplished there. I look back on the total experience with so much pride in the company we built, what we taught people about leadership, and the lives and careers we influenced around the world. My departure was a minor blip in an *overwhelmingly* positive experience.

And what I've learned is that when you adopt a learning perspective, that's how you come to see the failures.

. . .

If you want to maximize your potential in your life and career, you need to be willing to take risks that could lead to failure, and you need to analyze those failures honestly to extract as much learning as possible from each one. Then, you have to find a way to keep reminding yourself of the lessons you've already learned to make absolutely sure you don't repeat them. Learning from failure isn't the most fun way to learn, but as Mark Twain said, you will learn things you can't learn any other way.

Learning from Your Failures

- When was the last time you really picked apart your role in a failure? If you can't think of any, that's a sign that you should move on to the next question.

- When was the last time you took a risk that could result in failure—and more learning along the way?

- What's something you've learned from a failure that you were able to turn into a much greater success or achievement than the original goal?

Part Two

LEARN TO

Every now and then
a man's mind is stretched
by a new idea or sensation,
and never shrinks back to
its former dimensions.

—Oliver Wendell Holmes Sr.

Chapter 8

What Every Birdwatcher Knows

Soon after I became COO of Pepsi's beverage division, I went on a learning tour of our plants. I visited the Pepsi bottling plant in Baltimore. It was in a tough part of town and had a reputation for being one of our lowest-performing facilities. I knew this would be one of the best places to learn about our big operational challenges.

When I arrived, I was struck by the bullet holes scarring the Pepsi sign and the graffiti covering the building, but those were just cosmetic problems. The real problems were inside the building. This facility earned less money per case than any bottling plant we owned. When we had tried to address the issues with management, the leadership problems became obvious. They complained and pointed fingers. Nobody wanted to dive in and fix the real issues.

So I met with the sales and manufacturing teams and asked straight out, "What's working and what needs to be fixed?" They replied, "Nothing and everything." They weren't used to having executives ask their opinions, but when I encouraged them to elaborate and then shut my mouth, they had plenty to say—for two straight hours. "It takes the trucks forever to get out of here." "The fountain guys don't get the equipment they need." "The place is filthy." It was a real airing of grievances (and it was clear that the leaders had created a culture of complaining rather than active learning). But I just kept listening. *I* saw problems, too, but I resisted the urge to jump in—because under their complaints were a host of good ideas. The longer they talked, the longer I listened, the more ideas came to the surface.

Finally, one man said, "OK, you don't seem like such a bad guy. What are you going to do about all this?"

"I'm not going to do a damn thing," I said. They looked at me like I was crazy. "You know the problems better than anyone, so you should know the best way to fix them." Then I asked the plant manager to join us—I had intentionally not included him before. "These people have a lot of good ideas," I said, "and I want you to work with them. I'm coming back in six months to see the progress. When I do, I want to see all the people who are here now back in this room."

The day I returned the workers practically poured out the front door to greet me. They couldn't wait to show me all the improvements they had made, especially the changes they had implemented to make the truck-loading process more efficient. The place wasn't perfect, but it was *much* better than it had been. They were so proud of what they had accomplished, the problems they had solved, the ideas they had executed, and I was so proud of them, too.

And all of that happened because I listened (and convinced the plant manager to work with them).

Every year, one person or organization receives the Listener of the Year Award. It's a real award given by the International Listening Association (also real) to those who "epitomize the highest standards and principles of effective listening." In 2011, that person was Nancy Kline. After decades studying how to improve thinking, she determined that any of us can do two things to create an environment in which people think dramatically better: we can give others our full attention by listening at the highest level, and when that's not enough, we can ask incisive questions. (More on that in the next chapter.)

Nancy was lucky enough to grow up experiencing her mother's extraordinary listening skills, which might be why she was an award-winning listener herself. She described it in her book *Time to Think:*

Listening to Ignite the Human Mind. "My mother's listening was not ordinary. Her attention was so immensely dignifying, her expression so seamlessly encouraging, that you found yourself thinking clearly in her presence, suddenly understanding what before had been confusing, finding a brand-new, surprising idea. You found excitement where there had been tedium. You faced something. You solved a problem. You felt good again. . . . She simply gave attention. But the quality of that attention was catalytic."[1]

If it seems like I've been writing about listening in almost every chapter, I have. And you can expect to read more in the following chapters. There's simply no way to capture the full power of good listening in one chapter; it's core to every part of active learning. In this chapter, I simply want to emphasize two things that all active learners know:

- **You cannot learn if you cannot listen.**

- **Listening produces clearer thinking and better ideas and greater motivation for action, and that dramatically expands what we can achieve.**

The world is full of great ideas that are stuck in people's heads because nobody is making the time, space, or effort to really listen to them. When people are brave enough to share their ideas, passion, and insights, the very *least* you can do is listen. Better yet, you can listen *well*.

Larry Senn taught me a basic rule of listening: be here, now. Usually, we're not listening well because mentally we're somewhere else and some*time* else. Our thoughts are constantly shifting to the past or the future. We're thinking about the next meeting or an irritating conversation we had or an idea for solving the other person's problems or the clever reply we've been saving up. So often, when someone is speaking to us, we're thinking about what we want to say next rather than staying present and only listening—giving them room to fully explore and share their ideas before deciding how to respond. When you can be fully present, there in the moment with that person, you aren't just improving your own thinking, you're improving theirs, too.

Our egos also block good listening. Sometimes, we just don't like what people have to say, we're afraid that *we* might have to change based on what we hear, or we believe we already know what they have to share. You know from the last chapter that my most public failures were often a result of ideas that could have been much stronger—even successful— if I had only listened better. **Arrogance causes deafness, and one of the easiest traps to fall into when you've earned some success is forgetting to listen.**

Ken Chenault, former CEO of American Express, learned these lessons the not-so-easy way. He told me that in his mid-thirties, he thought of himself as a hard-charging, performance-focused leader who was also a good guy who treated people respectfully. But during a performance review, feedback from the people on his team suggested something else: *you're not a good listener.*

He resisted the feedback, thinking, "I'm nice to people." Luckily, the people on his team pushed back with a hefty dose of reality. They told him, "If you don't feel someone is saying something that is really impactful, you zone out. In fact, we have a term for it: the Ken Zone. . . . You only give us two minutes. If we don't say something that is on your agenda or that you think is really bright, you're out."

He was devastated, doubly so because he couldn't escape the truth of it. People felt disrespected and belittled, *and* he was missing important ideas. He realized the negative impact this was having on his success as a leader, so he focused on improving.

Three months later, he went back for more feedback, expecting a big improvement. That's not what his review showed. The problem with being a poor listener is that two people are involved. Ken had to change his behaviors *and* he had to change other people's perceptions of how much he cared, which takes time. He kept working on it. Finally, about five years later, somebody who worked with him said,

"Ken, one of the things that's really remarkable about you is you're such a good listener." And Ken said, "Let me tell you a story."

Like Ken, I've always thought of myself as a good listener, but I've fallen into the same traps. When I was still at Yum!, we created the Lead2Feed program. Middle and high school students in the program would form project teams to help solve hunger in their communities while learning essential leadership skills. When I left Yum!, the company discontinued the program, which often happens when new leaders come in with fresh ideas for having a positive impact. I wanted to keep the program going and make it even more successful, so the Lift a Life Novak Family Foundation took it over.

Although the infrastructure was there, we knew we had opportunities for improvement. We began listening to teachers and students around the country who could tell us what was working and what wasn't. A couple of years in, the teacher advisory committee raised a concern: the name was too limiting. They and their students saw more opportunities in their communities to have a greater positive impact beyond addressing hunger. They suggested changing the name to Lead4Change, explaining that more kids would be interested and more people in the communities would get involved.

I didn't listen—in fact, I shut it down. "We've got a great brand that we've been building for years," I said. "We'd be crazy to throw that away." Luckily, we had shown them that we valued their honest input, so they kept pushing the idea. Eventually, I recognized that I was letting an ego-driven internal voice convince me I was right. I made the choice to really *listen* instead—and I discovered that *they* were right. Changing the name has helped the program grow and reach more than 2 million students in its first decade.

We should take inspiration from birdwatchers, who often can't use any other sense *but* listening. They develop their ability to distinguish between subtle differences in notes and rhythms. They listen so that they know what to look for, not the other way around. **Active learners make the same effort—they avoid making assumptions about what they'll hear based on what they think they know.**

Tim Ryan, chairman of PwC, shared this powerful insight with me: "We often associate courage with taking a hill, and loud voices. Courage sometimes is a willingness to listen." That was certainly true in his experience. On July 5, 2016, Tim's first day as chairman and senior partner, Alton Sterling was shot in Dallas, Texas, while pinned to the ground by police officers. The next night, police shot Philando Castile during a traffic stop. The night after that, at a Black Lives Matter protest, Micah Xavier Johnson opened fire and killed five police officers and wounded seven others.

Something was happening in the country that Tim had to acknowledge. He brought his leadership team together and composed an email with a simple message: he recognized that people were concerned and were hurting. In the days that followed, hundreds of people responded, but for Tim, the one that stood out was this one: "When I came to work Friday morning, the silence was deafening." It hit Tim that at PwC, people weren't comfortable talking about race. And despite their years of work on diversity and inclusion, they hadn't developed a true understanding of what it was like to be a person of color in the workplace.

That's when a courageous listening plan came about. Tim decided to shut down operations for a day and spend the time having deep discussions about race. A *Fortune* 50 CEO told him it was going to blow up in his face. One of his closest friends in the firm called to say that that was *not* what he'd been elected to do (the chairman position is an elected one at PwC). But Tim believes in the power of listening, so he moved forward.

That day was a turning point for him and, in many ways, for the company. The company certainly didn't solve the problems of racial inequality and bias in America or even at PwC, but people listened, learned, and grew compassion and understanding, and that allowed them to move forward in a better way. And it spurred Tim to cofound CEO Action for Diversity & Inclusion, an organization where leaders could share best practices.

When we listen well, we can learn and expand our thinking. But sometimes, we end up motivating other people to reconsider *their* opinions or take different action. In psychologist Adam Grant's book *Think Again*, he describes how one doctor used good listening to change people's minds about essential vaccinations and how a volunteer peacekeeper used it to convince one of the world's most violent warlords to engage in peace talks. "Listening is a way of offering others our scarcest, most precious gift: our attention," he wrote. "Once we've demonstrated that we care about them and their goals, they're more willing to listen to us."[2] Good listening that engages people's minds begins with an attitude of humility, curiosity, and respect. It builds trust and connection, and helps people be more open.

I can't stress enough the essential nature of hearing what someone has to say, *especially* when it challenges your worldview or is even contradictory to what you believe to be true. Remember, truth-tellers are some of the most important people in our lives, because they help us grow and expand what's possible. And when they're more willing to listen to us, we're all more likely to learn something important, together.

Learning to Listen

- What have you learned at important moments in your life by making the effort to listen well?

- Try to think of a time when you listened with a level of attention so powerful that it changed how somebody thought or felt. What was different about that moment for them or for you? What was the result?

- Consider a moment when just talking out a problem helped the solution become suddenly obvious or substantially better. How did the other person (or people) listen well? What *didn't* they do?

Chapter 9

What If, How Could, and Why

Not long ago, my daughter, Ashley Butler, and I met with the doctor who leads the Wendy Novak Diabetes Institute, Kupper Wintergerst. He's been helping us develop the institute in partnership with the largest medical center in Louisville. We care about this, possibly more than anything else we've done through our foundation. As a family, we've learned through experience just how difficult the challenges of diabetes are. Our goals for the institute aren't small. We want it to provide all the resources families desperately need. We want it to provide cutting-edge treatment and exceptional results. We want it to change lives.

These were the goals we were discussing with Dr. Wintergerst. But at some point, I realized that the conversation had mostly focused on what *we* wanted and why this all mattered so much to *us*. Leading the kinds of programs that we were discussing would be a significant demand on top of the doctor's already intense schedule and his need to be with his family. He'd even mentioned the challenges of balancing work and family early in the meeting. If he didn't want to accomplish what we wanted to accomplish, as much as we wanted it, our team would face constant struggles. We wouldn't achieve our lofty goals.

I looked him in the eye and said, "Listen, I know we can fund this, and you can make it happen. But is this really what *you* want to do?"

I was asking him to consider why it mattered to him, and I was showing my interest and concern. Well, he just lit up. His passion and purpose meter jumped up to 10. And we learned exactly how much the institute would mean to him. He learned that what he wanted mattered to us, too. After the meeting, Ashley said, "You know, I think his commitment to our goals doubled just because you asked that question."

Active learners know that one of the best tools for learning is a well-aimed question.

I always tell people that the best thing about being new in any job, company, role, or project is that you have carte blanche to ask questions. It's the only way to learn. The trick is to be secure enough and curious enough to *keep* asking questions—as many as possible. "As questioners, we peak at about the age of four, which is a little sad when you think about it," explained Warren Berger, journalist and author of *A More Beautiful Question.* "At about that age, we ask hundreds of questions a day designed to advance our learning, our abilities." But as we age, we become overly confident in our knowledge or overly worried about looking like we don't know something.

"As you become more senior as a leader, it's even trickier to be curious—because you think you know a lot and other people think that you know a lot," Michael Bungay Stanier, author of the bestsellers *The Advice Trap* and *The Coaching Habit,* said to me. "But if you think to yourself, my role as a senior leader is to use my wisdom not to have the fast answer but to enable the others around me to figure out the problems, come up with their own solutions, and make sure that they're not doing anything stupid—if you bring your advice in at the right time—then you unlock something amazing." **Active learners make the effort to stay curious first and dole out advice second** so that they don't fall victim to what Michael calls the "Advice Monster," which grows from our need to tell it, save it, or control it. "All of them are impossible," he said. "It's impossible to know everything.

It's impossible to save everybody or everything. It's impossible to control everything."

Instead, active learners redirect that energy to keep exploring and discovering. When I was on the board of JPMorgan Chase, I was elected to compile the feedback from the board and give CEO Jamie Dimon his annual performance review because of my focus on people development. Jamie asked several questions about every piece of feedback I gave: "If the board thinks I should focus more on X, how can I get more efficient at Y?" "How do you think I could improve at this or that?" "What else am I missing in that area?" And Brian Cornell, the hugely successful CEO of Target, told me he fights to stay curious through literal language metrics. He tries to communicate in a question-to-statement ratio of 3:1.

A flood of poorly thought-out questions that don't advance your thinking or learning isn't the answer though. The key is to ask *better* questions. In my book *Taking People with You*, I taught the importance of asking questions that promote insight. Warren Berger believes the antidote is to ask *more beautiful questions*, which by his definition, "shift the way we perceive or think about something—and that might serve as a catalyst to bring about change." Nancy Kline, the winner of the Listener of the Year Award and author I mentioned in the previous chapter, uses the term "Incisive Questions": "Between you and a wellspring of good ideas is a limiting assumption," she wrote. "The assumption can be removed with an Incisive Question."[1]

A perfect example is the difference between asking, What *should* we do? and the more incisive, What *could* we do? Researchers have even studied the difference and found that **when we use "should," we limit everybody's thinking to the most obvious or safest options.[2] When we use "could," we open our minds to a broader world of possibility.** I used that technique when asking people how we could grow the business. People often think in terms of modest growth and develop plans to achieve it. I liked to ask, instead of shooting for 5 percent growth, how *could* we grow the company by 10 percent? (In part three, I'll share how simplifying to get to the most essential question delivers the most important insights.)

"What if" questions are a powerful way to kickstart people's imaginations and break away from limiting assumptions. When I'm trying to break away from my own assumptions, I often ask, "If some hotshot came in to take over my job, what would she do?" I love to ask, "What would you do if you had my job?" I've posed it to people from all backgrounds, from line cooks to corporate board members. You can't believe the insights that one question has generated over the years. A common answer I'd hear on the front lines was a diplomatic version of "I'd fire my boss." That helped me spot needed coaching and leadership development, and sometimes people who weren't a good culture fit. From restaurant managers, I'd hear things like, "I'd cut out half of the bureaucracy we have to deal with" or "I'd stop trying to reduce our food costs. It's getting in the way of producing good products." Asking those questions was a great way to let people know that I valued what they thought and what they cared about.

Whether you want to call them incisive questions, more beautiful questions, or questions that promote insight, active learners use them to get past the blocks and biases the brain creates, cut through the BS, and help people generate better thinking, better ideas, better learning.

Marvin Ellison, CEO of Lowe's, told me how important questions were for him when he was new to the company. He showed up one day at the Bullhead City, Arizona, store, a location where the average household income was about $35,000. Inside, he saw employees setting up a display for deck stain. Decks are expensive to build and maintain, and they don't do well in climates like Arizona, where more people have concrete or tile patios. Marvin introduced himself to the store manager and said, "I thought all of the patios here were concrete." The manager told him that was right. "So why are we setting up a display of deck stain?" That's what the corporate office told them to do, the manager said.

The next day at a store in a hot corner of Texas, Marvin noticed a patio display featuring a fire pit. Once again, he found the store manager and, this time, the district manager, too. "Why are we setting a display for a fire pit when it's 112 degrees outside?" Same answer: instructions from corporate.

Marvin kept encountering similar situations. That simple question, Why are we doing this?, uncovered a serious problem in the company: managers held a limiting assumption that they would get in trouble if they deviated from the product and promotion plans that came from corporate. They weren't empowered to make the best choice for each store. The insight led to intensive leadership training and an effort to develop a different cultural expectation.

I think incisive or beautiful questions start with the most basic: **Why do we do things a certain way or why do we think a certain way? And in what new way *could* we act or think that would help us solve a problem or achieve something better?** From there, we follow the rabbit trail with more questions to get to a deeper level of learning—and to show that we want to understand other people's thinking better.

I like to use questions when trying to uncover what I call "Slow No's." You're in a meeting and you're talking about a new strategy, like changing a process, a product, or a marketing tactic. Some people in the room don't want to do it or don't agree with the strategy, but they're not speaking up. The US Navy has a communication tactic, "Silence means consent," that it uses to minimize radio contact between ships at sea. In business and life, just the opposite is true; silence means *dis*sent or at least a lack of commitment. People don't want to say no or come across as obstinate, so they say nothing at all. These are the Slow No's, and they are the bane of making the right things happen. People leave the meeting misaligned. They don't have their head, heart, or hands committed, so there's limited follow-through or poor execution. The only way to sniff out the Slow No's is to ask better, direct questions that encourage people to share what they're really thinking, like, "Bill, what are your biggest concerns?" or "Ella, what effect will this have on your department?" Asking better questions gives people the room to confront their own biases or limiting assumptions.

As leaders, we all need good people around us willing to play this role for *us*, people who help improve our thinking and ideas. As we've seen over and over with some high-profile corporate failures, big problems can pop up when no one is questioning the people at the top. I'm not talking about only corruption and fraud; I'm also talking about making good decisions. Even leaders with the best of intentions can have dumb ideas. I've had my share, but one that I was saved from stands out.

When we were just launching Yum!, Andy Pearson, my partner and cofounder, assembled an all-star team for our board. I learned how important their contribution would be early on. At our second board meeting, I came in pumped up with enthusiasm for the new company and the big idea of building a new corporate headquarters. I wanted to create the look of a global market leader by having a new campus and a world-class training center. The board members didn't say no to the idea, but they did ask a lot of questions—not just what it would cost, but what we'd be getting for that money and why it would help the company.

Based on their questions, I went back to the team working on the project and began an entirely new discussion. We recognized that we had a functional headquarters, and it wouldn't look very good to spend money building a brand-new one while we were nearly $5 billion in debt (inherited in the spinoff from PepsiCo). The board helped me overcome the assumptions I had about what it would take to get people to believe in our new company—substance rather than style—by asking the right questions.

A last point: how we ask questions can be just as important as the questions we ask. Bonnie Hill, who was a Black female executive with companies like the Times Mirror Foundation and the *Los Angeles Times* at a time when there weren't many people like her in positions of leadership, shared some exceptional advice with me, which she received from a friend: **never discount the question you're going to ask.** Don't lead with, "This may be a dumb question, but . . ." or "I should probably already know this, but . . ." or "This might be wrong thinking, but . . ." It immediately allows people to discount you and to discount the importance of the question you're asking, so you'll end up learning a lot less.

To cap all of this wisdom, I'll turn to a quote often attributed (probably incorrectly) to the great questioner Albert Einstein: "If I had an hour to solve a problem and my life depended on the solution, I would spend the first fifty-five minutes determining the proper question to ask, for once I know the proper question, I could solve the problem in less than five minutes." It's a great reminder that if you begin by asking good questions, you'll learn what you need to know to take good action.

Learning to Ask Better Questions

- When in your life or work have you learned something powerful by asking a good question at the right time? Or when have you asked a question that produced a totally unexpected answer?

- Is there an area in your life where you feel confused or uncertain, or like a novice? If so, have you been asking enough questions to build your understanding?

- What one question could you ask today that could make a substantial difference in what you learn and in what you help others discover?

Chapter 10

Ditch the Blinders

Learn to make—and check—your own judgments

The words "trailer park" can conjure up all sorts of negative stereotypes—of poverty and ignorance, of kids in ratty clothing and weeds growing up through a mobile home's supports. I've experienced those stereotypes. When I tell people that I grew up in trailer courts, I can see their assumptions in how their expressions change: I must have had a disadvantaged youth or I've had limited experience of the world.

But their images and assumptions have nothing to do with the reality of my childhood. In many ways, I can't imagine having had a more idyllic upbringing or a more expansive view of the world *because* I grew up in trailer parks—in a new town every few months until I was twelve. But it has also taught me to be highly sensitive to stereotyping and assumptions, especially about people, *and* to make my own assessment of new people and environments. Throughout my career, this has helped me avoid making unwarranted or snap judgments. I've learned that most people have something valuable to offer if you keep an open mind.

Unconscious bias is a killer of effective communication, good ideas, and important learning, because we discount the people or circumstances behind them. The human brain is a logic machine, and it tries to overcome ambiguity wherever it finds it—to make decision-making easier and life feel a little safer. It likes to categorize things. It likes to develop heuristics, or mental shortcuts. It relies on templates that are based on past experiences. Then, as Stephen Klemich and Mara Klemich explained in *Above the Line*, when something similar shows up in front of you, it "pulls up the old template, says 'Close enough,' and overlays that experience onto the present moment."[1] With that template comes memories, thoughts, emotions, even physical sensations. The problem is that "close enough" often isn't very close, especially if our experiences are limited. And that's when our thinking becomes an obstacle rather than a tool. That's when we fall victim to limiting prejudgments that can cut off the flow of good ideas in our lives.

If the brain didn't develop these categories, shortcuts, and templates, we'd barely be able to make a decision about how to leave a room because we wouldn't have a doorknob shortcut stored away. But **active learners consciously work to avoid relying on assumptions, blanket categorizations, and limiting templates—their own and others'.**

How? Well, the previous two chapters on listening and asking better questions are a good start. But even before that comes exposure. You have to talk to people—lots of different people and especially people you might not typically interact with—and put yourself in different circumstances, where you can see people in action. This habit helps expand your experiences so that your templates and categories are broader and more encompassing, and your decision-making and judgments are more flexible.

Growing up moving from town to town every three months helped me develop my own expanded perspective of the countless people I met and my own gut instincts. Either I could assume that what people told me was true, or I could make the effort to talk to people, learn about them, and decide for myself.

During those years, my mother was concerned about what all the moving was doing to my education, a concern she shared with my teacher in Dodge City, Kansas, Mrs. Anschultz, who quickly eased her worries. "David is not even out of the fourth grade, and he has already lived in more places than most of these kids will visit in their lifetimes," Mrs. Anschultz said. "Your son is getting the best education of anybody I know." I was getting exposure—to different places, different people, and different experiences I might never have had in a more typical upbringing. For example, in one school, I was one of just a few white kids. It taught me how uncomfortable it can be to be in the minority, and I often remembered those months when working with someone who found themselves in a similar situation.

Ray Scott, president and CEO of Lear Corporation, which makes seating and electronics systems for many cars worldwide, is proud to have grown up in Flint, Michigan. When he was young, his family lived in a tough part of town, and he told me that those experiences taught him to stay humble. They didn't help him when he moved to Sweden, though, where he was responsible for fixing a struggling business line, an experience he now describes as one of the most challenging of his career. He went in with the attitude, *I'm the American. I know what to do. We're gonna get back on track and be successful.* "I had a mindset of how I was going to lead, and I had no respect for the Swedish culture or the people and their understanding of how you motivate and inspire."

Ray's troubles began immediately. Sweden has a strong egalitarian culture, and he wasn't letting people participate in the fix. He wasn't letting people be heard. But he kept pushing forward, thinking that the division hadn't been successful, and he knew how to change all that. Every day, he received notifications of grievances employees had submitted to the union.

> When he offered an especially talented team member a promotion, the manager said, "I don't want to be promoted."
>
> "What do you mean?" Ray said, incredulous that this person was turning down the chance to move up and oversee the other program managers.

"I have everything I want. I'll still do the job."

Ray said, "No, you have to manage it. There has to be a hierarchy. I want to make sure you're responsible. You get a car."

"Why do I want a car?"

"Because you get to come to work in a car."

"I have a bike."

"But it rains here all the time."

"Ray, there's no bad weather; there are just poorly dressed people."

"You'll get more money."

"I don't want more money. I'll be considered different from my friends."

Recalling that interaction, Ray told me, "It made me realize that I was very one-dimensional." The experience taught him to have much greater respect for the power of culture, life experiences, and individual perspectives. He lets that guide how he runs Lear today, especially in his focus on diversity—because diverse perspectives grow a stronger, more resilient organization with better results. It's why I've always believed in the idea of unity in values but diversity in style, to encourage people to bring their unique perspectives to work.

Active learners recognize that *everybody* has bias and prejudice, their own categories and templates and ways of seeing the world. They work on overcoming their own, but they also don't blindly trust the opinions they hear from others. They make their own judgments based on what they learn. They work to overcome the "spotlight effect." Chip Heath and Dan Heath used that phrase in their book *Decisive* to describe our tendency to give too much weight to the information right in front of us, which leads to conclusions or snap decisions without considering information just outside the spotlight. When somebody we know and trust tells us, "This is how it is" or "This is who this person is," it's easy to accept and stop looking beyond that. But we need to move the spotlight around and look for more information if we want to make our own best judgments.

When I led large companies, I would regularly find someone sitting alone in the lunchroom and ask if I could join them. Once that person got past the initial surprise of a senior leader asking to eat lunch with them, conversation would flow. Every time, I learned something that I didn't know before I got there. A young marketing person gave me good ideas about how to train new employees based on his own experience as the new guy. Sometimes I would learn how people felt about decisions we were making and where we were headed as a company. More than that, I expanded my experience of the people who worked for our company to challenge my categories, shortcuts, and templates.

As CEO of Yum!, I also had the privilege of touring our restaurants often, meeting frontline workers who were just as smart as I was but who hadn't had the same opportunities. Because they happened to be washing dishes, working the drive-through, or standing at a grill, people automatically assumed that they didn't have much to say worth listening to. It was a big mistake that I always tried to rectify, and it saved us from making mistakes more than once. It's also how I brought to life the defining principle of Yum!'s culture: a culture where everyone makes a difference. For instance, when we launched our oven-roasted chicken pieces at KFC, everyone at our corporate office thought the product was just great as it was. But then I talked to the cooks at a couple of our restaurants who showed me how difficult it was to make the product with consistent results in the real world. That insight sent us back to the drawing board. Thanks to those cooks, we found a quicker and simpler process for making a consistently good product, which saved us a ton of time and money in the long run.

Bernie Marcus, who cofounded Home Depot, would do the same when he was CEO. He opened himself up to the associates on the front line, often asking, "How would you tackle this?" or "How would you do that?" It's how he gathered some incredibly valuable ideas that helped Home Depot grow as fast as it did.

Before you can **check your judgment about the ideas people share, you first must check the assumptions you're making that limit the people who are in your sphere of influence.** For instance, when she became president and CEO of IBM, Ginni Rometty could see three transformations the company needed to make. It needed a new technology platform, it needed new skills, and it needed to change how it worked as an organization. (You know, just the small stuff!) The hardest to solve was acquiring skilled talent—because the people doing the acquiring were operating on two faulty assumptions: people with at least a bachelor's degree and with experience would be better hires. But IBM desperately needed digital skills and couldn't get them. There just weren't enough trained people in the talent pool. Technology also changes dramatically every three to five years, and IBM had too many people who weren't all that interested in changing with it.

So, Ginni helped the team make two big hiring changes. First, they started looking at high schools and community colleges for talent and doing more in-house training and education for the skills they needed most. Second, they started testing for the traits that made people successful through transformation: curiosity, grit, and drive. When they let go of their assumptions and biases about degrees, background, and experience, they found people who could bring the greatest value to the organization.

We all make prejudgments in our life and work, and none of us likes to admit we're doing it. The current conversations about inequality, discrimination, and exclusion in our country highlight this fact. But we still do it. We do it about strangers and friends, people we dislike and people we love. For example, I went to lunch with an older friend who is semiretired from leading his family business. He was telling me about his concerns that his son wasn't seeking his counsel or wasn't leveraging the knowledge he had shared to solve some key problems. "I think it's chronological snobbery," he said, using a term C. S. Lewis introduced to capture "the uncritical acceptance of the intellectual climate common to our own age and the assumption that whatever has gone out of date is on that account discredited."[2] No, I wouldn't take medical advice from a doctor who was trained in 1920, but I also know that some of the best business advice I've ever received came from people who were decades older than me, who had come up during very different eras of leadership.

This is why it's so important to build your self-awareness. When you understand who you are, how you operate, and where you might be letting biases and assumptions rule (because we all do sometimes), you'll be in a better position to understand and check your judgment.

The more you make the effort to learn about diverse ideas and worldviews from more diverse people, the deeper and more robust your learning will be, and the more effective action you'll be able to take with it.

Learning to Make—and Check—Your Own Judgments

- Take a minute to consider whether you're making a prejudgment somewhere in your life or work right now. This isn't easy. Try considering a situation that feels limiting or an idea that maybe you've shot down because of who proposed it. What's the assumption or bias behind the judgment? What could you do to test your assumptions?

- How could you broaden your templates by interacting with and learning about more people, their ideas, and their experiences?

- Have you ever accepted somebody else's judgment blindly, without seeking out more perspectives or learning more on your own, and then regretted it later on? What would you have done differently?

Learn to see
the world the
way it really is

Chapter 11

Are You Delusional?

Shortly after Wendy and I got engaged, I went to Louisville to meet her parents. She was anxious to know what kind of impression I'd made, so at the first opportunity, she pulled her mother aside and said, "So, what do you think?" At that moment they could hear me trash-talking her two brothers, Jeff and Rick, as we played basketball in the driveway.

"Well," my future mother-in-law, Anne, replied, "he's a very loud man."

She was right. Wendy says I'm like a big puppy dog, jumping around, barking, and wagging its tail. When you're in a position of leadership, that kind of enthusiasm can get you into trouble because people confuse it with excessive optimism, even delusion. They can assume you don't want to hear about the bubble-bursting realities of a situation—even if all you want is the truth.

Here's an example: I'm incredibly proud of my podcast, *How Leaders Lead*. I think the conversations are inspiring and helpful to leaders around the world. Ask me about it, and you'll hear (and see) my enthusiasm pour out. After building it for a year, we hired an experienced podcast producer and brand builder, Tim Schurrer, who is now the CEO of David Novak Leadership, to help us improve it. During one meeting, when we were still getting to know each other, I asked him how we could improve. I could tell he was hemming and hawing. He gave me vague answers. I finally said, "Tim, the only thing I care about is getting to the best possible product. What do you think we should do?" That made it safe for him to give me the reality: compared to other highly successful podcasts, he said, our intros and outros just weren't good enough. We weren't drawing people in with a big idea to get them excited, and we weren't leaving them with a clear takeaway. It was hurting our audience engagement. "OK," I said. "What do we do to fix it?" He gave us a better model, we implemented it right away, and it made our podcast better.

Active learners deal in reality. They recognize an essential truth: **delusional people don't learn well**. They work hard to follow the often-repeated advice of my mentor at Yum!, Andy Pearson: **learn to see the world the way it really is, not how you wish it to be.** If you assume that the best ideas and soundest knowledge are based in reality, what are the chances that you're going to be open to them if you're clinging to what you *wish* rather than acknowledging what *is*? And how can you possibly know where or how to grow and learn if you don't know your starting point?

Unfortunately, we *don't* usually see the world the way it really is. Our brains create stories (rooted in those categories, templates, and heuristics I described in the last chapter) about everything we perceive, based on our experiences, desires, and expectations. Along the way, when information seems to be missing or contradictory, the brain fills in gaps or makes choices about what information to use or discard. (Surprise, surprise, it really likes information that proves the story right, a problem called confirmation bias.) An example that neuroscientists point to all the time is the divergent stories different people will tell after witnessing the same event. They'll swear that what they saw was the truth, even though it often isn't, or at least not the whole truth. Optical illusions are the visual manifestation of the brain filling in the gaps. The brain interprets the information it receives in a certain way, and we can't unsee it, even though we know it's not the truth or reality.

Basically, it's easy to be a little delusional. Long before neuroscientists could begin to describe how we process information and create meaning from it, great philosophers and thinkers knew it was a challenge. In the early twentieth century, the influential lawyer Clarence Darrow said, "Man does not live by truth, but by the illusions that his brain conceives."[1]

So, what's an active learner to do? Well, here's what else Darrow said: "Chase after the truth like all hell and you'll free yourself, even though you never touch its coat tails."[2]

I'm a little more optimistic. I think we can get close to the truth in many situations. It starts by inviting more truth-tellers into your life who will keep orienting you to reality. But you can't make your perception of reality somebody else's responsibility (or base your judgments on their judgments). **If you want to see the world the way it really is, you've got to hunt for the truth. You've got to chase it like all hell.**

A good starting point is to pull in as much *objective* information as possible and then test it against the ideas and opinions you're hearing. Are those ideas and opinions based on wishes and desires or are they based on the facts? Are they whole truths or half-truths? Do the people behind them *think* or do they *know*? Do they *reveal* blind spots or cover them up? What I'm really talking about here is critical and analytical thinking. Today, with all the information flying at us, this is more important than ever.

In their book *Decisive*, Chip Heath and Dan Heath explained that a sound decision-making *process* is more important than data and analysis, because no matter what, that data or our analysis of it is often flawed. We interpret it based on what we wish or what we assume or what we think, not what *is*.

They described the work of two decision-making researchers, Dan Lovallo and Olivier Sibony, who studied more than a thousand corporate decisions and how they were produced. "When the researchers compared whether process or analysis was more important in producing good decisions—those that increased revenues, profits, and market share—they found that 'process mattered more than analysis—by a factor of six.'"[3] Good process can lead to better analysis, they explained, but analysis without good process won't produce the best learning. You need both to orient yourself to reality.

One analysis-process combo we used to use at Yum! was a problem detection study. We asked customers to tell us all the things that were wrong in a specific category, such as a new product that was received poorly, or drive-through lines that were too long. Then we discussed the problems, ranked them in order of importance and how frequently they occurred, and then dug deeper for possible solutions. The magic happened when we solved the most important problems that occurred most frequently. That was always the path to turning a business around or making a huge leap in market share.

When you see the world the way it really is, the right action becomes very clear.

In 2000, Taco Bell unveiled two new menu items—the grilled stuffed burrito and the quesadilla. They were tasty and would appeal to different customer segments. We were sure (always a dangerous word) same-store sales would grow as the new items showed up in restaurants. But market tests (our *analysis*) were dismal. Our customers weren't buying them. We had to get to the root cause, so we used a *process* to understand *why* they were dismal. We launched a problem detection study for the Taco Bell brand and found out that the biggest problem we had was one of perception. Customers thought our products were messy. That's a huge problem when 70 percent of your business is drive-through. Nobody wants to show up somewhere after lunch with salsa stains on their shirt or a lap full of taco shell crumbs.

With our bubble burst and a clearer sense of reality, we reset. What matters most when you're eating food on the go? Portability. So we created a new ad campaign around our quesadilla, repositioning it as the "hottest new handheld." We even got Jeff Bezos to star in a commercial for it (you can find it on YouTube). We repositioned the grilled stuffed burrito as the "affordable heavy duty portable." The portability campaigns were immediately and fantastically successful—so successful that we decided to create a new travel-ready crunchy product, the Crunch Wrap, and position it as "Good to Go." We also knew most people thought of burgers as the ultimate on-the-go food, so we created a new tagline: "Think Outside the Bun."

Those products and campaigns produced almost double-digit growth in sales across the country. And all we had to do was acknowledge our customers' reality and orient ourselves to it—through process and analysis.

One of the best ways to be a better critical thinker is to make sure that your information is as close to the source as possible. If you don't go to the source yourself, you might be letting one perception after another influence what you end up hearing or learning. You won't know if you're seeing reality. At Yum! we taught the idea of "turn left first" in our "customer-mania" training for all leaders. Whenever they walked into a restaurant, they should first turn left and go talk to customers, rather than going straight to the back of the store to talk to managers or team members.

The late Ray Odierno, four-star general and former chief of staff of the US Army, used this strategy when assessing and coaching his leaders. Instead of asking people what kind of leader a person was or how the unit was performing, he visited the unit and attended its briefings. "I could tell when a leader had empowered his subordinates," he told me. When they were briefing, they were involved, they understood exactly what was going on, they weren't afraid to say things. It was an open, happy environment, and the people in it were more innovative and were better problem-solvers. He could also quickly spot signs that a unit wasn't performing well or a leader wasn't leading well. "Only the commander can talk. Everybody looks like they're falling asleep. They're not really happy. They're not involved." Odierno went to the source to assess the reality, which is especially important in a naturally hierarchical organization.

When you're trying to see the world the way it really is, **it's important to not be blinded by good news,** something a good process can help you overcome. A common adage you hear in sports is that a team is never as good as it looks when it's winning and never as bad as it looks when it's losing. The truth is often in the middle—the reality for most situations in life and business. But when we're winning, it's even easier to fall victim to confirmation bias and assume everything is just great.

Jamie Dimon, the legendary CEO of JPMorgan Chase and a former board member at Yum!, constantly compares his companies to best-in-class performers within the financial industry. He cares about internal improvement, of course, but in good times or bad, he wants to know how they compare to other successful companies in the industry on key measures. Your competition can be a great source of reality-based information. You can spot the companies that track it and those that don't. Sears didn't look to Walmart's success to understand the shifting realities of its market or customer needs, and Sears died. Leaders at Walmart pay a lot of attention to what they can learn from what's happening at Target, and vice versa, and they're *both* thriving.

We rated and ranked all of our restaurants, from top to bottom, on key performance measures. Those reminders of reality drove healthy competition. We also benchmarked ourselves against our competition on key customer measures. I loved working in a category where the market leader was doing well. It gave us a simple and vivid reality to check ourselves against.

People often say that Jamie has incredible instincts and that his gut-based judgment calls are the source of his success. When I asked him about it, he said, "I'm a nerd. I study and read everything. We work the numbers, the models, the facts. I look at history. I do *all* of that. . . . Sometimes the good answers are waiting to be found. And the way you find them is you work it." It's that combination of analysis, process, and experience that creates good gut instincts, he explained.

A great way to stay grounded is to not only chase the truth but also deal in it. Active learners know the value of being honest and transparent. **They tell it like it is, because they know when they**

do, there's a greater chance others will, too. That's precisely how Jamie runs his companies and why he is so respected and trusted.

That lesson became especially important to Yum! in November 2006. The day before our annual meeting with Wall Street analysts, we learned that people had gotten sick with *E. coli* in four states in the Northeast. Local health departments had tracked the source of those illnesses to Taco Bell. This was a terrible ordeal for those who got sick, and it frightened the public. Even though the problem was isolated to produce supplied to the Northeast, sales declined dramatically all over the country.

The first thing we did when we heard the news was work with the government to find the source of the illnesses. Tracing an illness is a tricky and cumbersome scientific process. It's difficult to rush it, and the pace can be frustrating when you're running restaurants. Before we had time to get all the facts, we had to give our presentation to investors, the same morning the outbreak appeared in both the *New York Times* and the *Wall Street Journal*.

The lesson we were reminded of that day is this: deal in reality and people trust you more and have more faith in your ideas or plans. I had our head of investor relations open the meeting by laying out everything we knew about the crisis and saying that we thought the press had done a good job reporting it. Surprisingly, when it came to the question-and-answer part of the program, nobody asked about the crisis. Because we were so obviously dealing in reality—acknowledging it, digging for more of it, and sharing it—our stock actually went up. And we took better action. The reality we uncovered is that the *E. coli* was brought in on lettuce, so we developed new and better processes for washing our produce.

Finally, when reality kicks you in the pants, it doesn't pay to resist it or deny it. Oscar Munoz, CEO of United Airlines, told me that early in his career, he had moved from PepsiCo, where he was a fast-rising star, to the Coca-Cola Company. He was young, still in his twenties, and felt pretty good about himself. At his new gig, he thought the Coke culture and leaders were a bit staid or conservative compared to PepsiCo, where younger, hard-charging people held higher leadership positions. It was Atlanta culture versus New York culture. During one of his first performance reviews, his boss gave him the gift of reality. "He did this magical thing," Oscar told me. "He took the HR document, folded it, and pushed it to the side. He said, 'Now if I could, just as friends, share a couple of things.' So I'm thinking, he probably wants me to date his daughter. . . . He said, 'You know, you're really good at what you do. And if there's one bit of feedback I would give you, it's that you're not yet as good as *you think* you are.'" That simple reality check helped Oscar realize that he still had plenty to learn from the people he worked with, and he'd be crazy to discount their experience. Sometimes, a reality check can be hard to swallow, but it always helps us learn more of the right things.

This is important, so I'm going to repeat it: **delusional people don't learn well.** They aren't great problem-solvers. They often don't follow the best course of action. And they can miss out on some of the most important opportunities. So, chase after the truth like all hell and you'll give yourself a special learning—and life—superpower.

Learning to See the World the Way It Really Is

- Think of a time when you felt you *finally* understood the reality of a situation. What did you see or learn that you had been missing until then? How did it change things for you going forward?

- How could getting closer to reality help you learn something vital in your life right now? A good sign is that you feel confused, unsure, or incapable of change. What about your analysis or process is keeping you from getting there?

- Where in your life are you relying on information that is secondhand, that just confirms your thinking, or that isn't capturing the whole truth of a situation—and how could you get to the truth or the source instead?

Chapter 12

Learn to develop pattern thinking

Making
1 + 1 = 3

Early in my career, when I was still working for an ad agency, I was promoted to managing supervisor for the Frito-Lay account, which included one of its biggest brands, Doritos. I was on the team charged with finding ideas for new flavors.

The original Doritos flavor was toasted corn. Nacho Cheese flavor followed, a big hit and an obvious extension: take the dip and put it on the chip. But when we began our research for the next great flavor, we started by looking down aisles *other than* the chip aisle, aisles that could point us in the direction of broader flavor trends. We found what we needed in salad dressing.

The bottled-salad-dressing business is about creating taste sensations so potent that they might overwhelm everything they're put on. That big, bold flavor is what we wanted for Doritos. Ranch was the top-selling salad-dressing flavor at the time, so we thought, "Why not put it on a chip?"

We also needed a name that would appeal to customers and be unique. For example, we could have called the first new Dorito "Cheese Doritos." But we called it "Nacho Cheese Doritos" to give it that something extra, an ad tactic called adding a unique image to a known quantity.

Ranch Doritos weren't going to cut it. Our unique image was about flavor *and* attitude: *Cool* Ranch Doritos were born, still a fan favorite all these years later.

The Cool Ranch process we went through reveals the power of pattern thinking. **Pattern thinking is 1 + 1 = 3 kind of learning. You create something bigger than its parts by pairing things that aren't obviously related** but that together create something new, exciting, and powerful. You need to discover the subtle similarities between two things that seem different on the surface and then make a leap to a new idea, interpretation, or action.

To prepare to make that leap, active learners expose themselves to as many patterns from as many disciplines as they can. Being curious about the world around us in the hope that we'll discover a new way of thinking about a problem or a new way of seeing an opportunity is core to active learning. Active learners read, listen, travel, try new things, explore hobbies and interests. They explore trends and insights from different disciplines, industries, cultures. Then they apply what they've absorbed to problems or goals. Those habits have helped me come up with some of my most successful ideas.

You might think of a pattern-thinking moment as an aha moment or a stroke of inspiration, but active learners don't wait for the moment to hit them; they work to find it. They develop the habit of seeking it. Peter Georgescu, chairman emeritus of advertising giant Young & Rubicam and author of *The Source of Success*, said of pattern thinking, "A creative solution is a leap, and that leap is supported and fed and nurtured by experiences in life. The richer your life experience is, the more creative you'll become." In his book, he offered this advice to hone your pattern thinking:

Practice and refine the skill of finding patterns of unconnected events in the world of human experience. This can be learned. Pattern recognition is one of the consistent elements of successfully creative business problem solvers. Insights can come from any direction if you hone this ability. Once, while reading

an article in the *Washington Post* on the Aztec irrigation system that brought water to dry, barren fields in Mexico, I had
a sudden recognition about how to help restructure my agency's direct marketing organization. Stories abound in business
about how enormously successful products, from Post-it notes
to Viagra, were discovered by seeing a popular application
of something originally developed for a completely different
purpose.[1]

You can see more examples of pattern thinking in creative and
innovative solutions throughout history. R. Buckminster Fuller, an
architect, designer, and innovator, based one of his greatest architec-
tural inventions, the geodesic dome, on structural patterns he saw in
nature. He believed that design principles in nature should influence
all our work because they've already evolved to be optimal. The idea
for Velcro came to Swiss engineer George de Mestral in 1948 when
he got home after a walk with his dog and discovered they were both
covered in cockleburs.

Some of our greatest creations emerged from pattern thinking
without the creator ever realizing it, though. Temple Grandin, autism
activist, and Richard Panek, award-winning science writer, described
the phenomenon in *The Autistic Brain*. For instance, mathematicians
have analyzed the work of great composers and found geometric patterns in their rhythms, octave shifts, and note progressions: "The
composers, of course, don't think of their compositions in these terms.
They're not thinking about math. They're thinking about music. But
somehow, they are working their way toward a pattern that is math-
ematically sound, which is another way of saying that it's universal."[2]
It doesn't stop with music. "Vincent van Gogh's later paintings had all
sorts of swirling, churning patterns in the sky—clouds and stars that
he painted as if they were whirlpools of air and light. And, it turns
out, that's what they were!" Modern physicists compared van Gogh's
patterns with the mathematical formula for turbulence in liquids and
found that they were almost identical.

Whether it happens on purpose or intuitively, pattern thinking emerges when we focus on being a multidisciplinary learner. Roger Goodell, commissioner of the NFL, is a good example. He takes regular trips to Silicon Valley because he sees it as a hotbed of the newest and most innovative ideas in business. He told me he's looking for "a new perspective and understanding of what's happening in technology and with companies. We don't just go see companies that we'll likely do business with. We actually see companies that we admire, that are finding new solutions out there using their technology, their products. And we try to see how we can apply that to ourselves, and how we can make the NFL better." Wi-Fi access in stadiums came to the NFL earlier than it did in many organizations in part due to these trips.

Active learners seek out patterns—*actively*. Roger *hunts* for a pattern that will help connect the dots to a breakthrough idea. Just as we hunted the salad-dressing aisle and found Cool Ranch Doritos. And just as Tom House, the renowned baseball pitching coach who is often called "the father of modern pitching mechanics," does. When he worked with the San Diego Padres, head trainer Dick Dent had players run football pass patterns to work their arms, get in some running, and mix up training sessions. Tom did the same and soon recognized a pattern. "I saw that all my elite pitchers threw the football perfectly. And the guys with bad mechanics couldn't make a spiral and didn't have any accuracy." It made him wonder what he could learn if he started working with quarterbacks. He filmed some of the best, including Joe Montana and Dan Marino. "We checked the biokinetics aerial model . . . and as it turned out, quarterbacks have exactly the same mechanics as a pitcher."

Those mechanics became the core of Tom's training, and he applied it to help pitchers stay on the mound into their forties. He then made the leap to working with football players. He met with Bill Belichick and explained that with a focus on the right mechanics and the right training regimen, he could help Tom Brady extend his career. And we all know Brady played at a high level until he finally retired at forty-five.

I think the most important and fundamental patterns can be applied across industries and disciplines, across boundaries and cultures. They're like the design principles Buckminster Fuller searched for in nature. For example, one of my great frustrations in life is lousy leadership. If you dig into the data, you'll see near-universal dissatisfaction with most leaders. I've seen the potential that's squandered by poor leadership, and I've seen what's possible with great leadership. This is the problem I've wanted to solve for the past few decades. It's why I taught the "Taking People With You" program when I led Yum! Brands and why I wrote a book based on it. Because I saw a pattern. Of the more than 1 million people who worked at Yum! worldwide, very few had received any real leadership education in their lives.

I began to look at other successful education initiatives and realized that most of them start quite early. *Why are we waiting to teach people how to lead when they're in their twenties or thirties or forties?* I asked. And then, What if I could inject the ideas in my program into education that's already happening—in middle schools and high schools? From that came the Lead2Feed program, which I described in chapter 8. (It's now Lead4Change.) But we didn't stop there. That success led me to wonder, Why couldn't we do something similar for college students? And that's how we created the Novak Leadership Institute at the University of Missouri. Take a successful leadership development program, add the infrastructure of schools and the passion of teachers who want to get students involved in their communities, and you get something bigger than the whole of its parts.

The best patterns to leverage are those that seem universal, like mathematical principles. When we were developing the Yum! culture after we launched in 1997, plenty of people told me it was impossible for us to have one culture for the company that we could apply around the globe, especially because I wanted to inject energy and fun into it. The international division was particularly resistant. The feeling was that you can't transfer values because values are local, and cultures are different. But then Peter Hearl, the executive VP of our international division, said to me, "Look, David, I've traveled all over the world, worked in multiple countries, and that's absolute bull. Good values are universal. We need to have one culture for everyone in the company, no matter where they are." We found a way to build a culture based on universal values that allowed for local adaptation and style, and it was crucial to our success. We proved that some patterns can create a leap forward despite boundaries, borders, and customs.

Just by reading this book, you're developing your pattern thinking. You might have zero interest in becoming CEO of a global corporation or commissioner of the NFL, and you might know nothing about baseball, but the experiences of all the people in these pages will influence your thinking. And as a result, you just might discover a breakthrough that helps you achieve whatever it is you *do* want to do.

Learning to Develop Pattern Thinking

- The last time you came up with an especially creative idea or solution, what was your inspiration? What pattern were you applying and where had you discovered it?

- How much time do you spend exploring outside your usual work and life experiences? Where are you getting exposure to different disciplines or industries?

- Think of a challenge you're facing or a problem you've been struggling to solve. Have you looked for patterns or ideas from unusual sources yet? If not, where could you turn next?

Chapter 13

The Stillness That Leads to Action

The first time Wendy suggested that I check out a local church after we moved to Louisville, Kentucky, I said, "Not interested." It wasn't that I didn't hold any religious beliefs; I just didn't see what attending services had to offer. I had some strong, preconceived notions about the experience and didn't want to spend my Sunday mornings getting a lecture.

"I think you'll like this church," she insisted. She had been attending for a few weeks. She knows me better than anybody, so I agreed to give it a try.

The first sermon I heard there was about having a vision for the future, and how important it is when trying to build a meaningful life. This was in 1995, early on in my tenure as the president of KFC, and that's exactly what we were working on. Without a positive, inspiring vision, we wouldn't be able to grow a strong company. It seemed like a sermon tailor-made for me. So, I showed up the following Sunday . . . and had the same experience. In fact, every time I went, it seemed like the sermon was just for me, covering a topic I was struggling with at work or in life.

I hold Christian beliefs, but I understand that not everybody does. I'm not trying to convince you to attend my church. I recognize that my experience of it has more to do with me and what I have needed in my life than the church itself. Beyond the perspective from the sermons, attending services created the opportunity to bond with people, and it offered insight into the local community and how we might get involved. But possibly the greatest benefit, and what I believe we are all in need of, was the time and space it created in my life for deep reflection.

It's difficult to have a learning perspective on the world without developing a practice of reflection. Many, many of the active learners I've known throughout my life make reflection a priority, a habit—whether it's through the practice of their faith, through meditation, or simply sitting quietly. They learn more about themselves, about others, and about the world by blocking out time to ponder ideas or challenges deeply. It's one reason Google had its 20 percent rule for years—the expectation that people will spend 20 percent of their time away from the demands of their day job exploring interesting ideas, learning new skills, or thinking about the future and what could be possible for the company.

About nine years ago, I discovered that other people in my network were on a similar spiritual path, and I joined a Monday morning Bible study group. It's a remarkable part of my week. It gives us all a safe place to share what we're struggling with or what's working in our lives, to explore our gratitude for what we've been given, and to examine our responsibility to do good in the world. The discussion forces deep thinking and self-examination—both in short supply for most of us. We learn from each other, we draw insight from the passages we discuss, and we push ourselves to *reflect,* honestly and openly.

In *The Way of Gratitude*, Galen Guengerich, the leader of All Souls Unitarian Church in New York City, writes, "If you have ever sought a deeper sense of your life's meaning, a more compelling understanding of your life's purpose, or a more engaging experience of joy," then you are a spiritual seeker.[1] That's not a label many people are comfortable with, even though it can mean anything you like. Galen shared a story about having dinner with a group of young adults who had found their way to his church. He asked them what had drawn them there and what they told friends about the experience or why they began attending. "Their answer was unanimous," he wrote. "'We don't say anything. It's not acceptable among young people our age, at least in New York City, to be part of a religious community. Our friends would think we're deluded and crazy.' . . . More and more people view spirituality as something individuals can pay attention to if they wish. But it's not something that should be practiced collectively and certainly not in public."

If you agree with that statement, or think the kind of spiritual exploration I've described isn't for you, consider this question: **Where in your life are you making time for honest, vulnerable *conversations* about what you value, about your purpose, about how you're giving back to the world and living your values?** These kinds of collective reflections could be some of the most powerful in terms of what you learn about yourself and others and how to expand the possibilities in your life. We're uncomfortable with them, though. They're on a level with talking about money. Not many of us make space or time for them.

Even at work, where we're supposed to be creative and thoughtful, making time for simple reflection alone or in small groups isn't common. Juliet Funt, author of *A Minute to Think*, described the challenge of trying to produce high-value work in days packed with meetings, calls, and tasks, with no time to sit quietly and think. "It doesn't work," she told me, "and that's why everyone works at night, and on the weekend, and early in the morning, and in a torturous extra shift after the kids go to bed." There was a time when you might see a leader in their office, kicked back and staring out the window (something I used to make time for in my schedule) and think "this is the golden hour, they're cooking the future of the business, they're writing our story." Now, the response is different. Thoughtfulness is a hidden thing that people sneak away to accomplish, because "if you try to think in a regular office," Juliet said, "somebody is going to come up to you and say, 'What are you doing? What are you doing? What are you doing?'"

Active learners fight the tendency to pack every moment of their day. They love quiet time. For instance, I love to be on an airplane, unreachable. It's a time when I do some of my most powerful thinking, when I have aha moments, when I commit to making big changes. I also create quiet time each morning. I write down gratitudes in a journal. I read a proverb and reflect on its meaning. It's those quiet moments that propel you forward. **It's the stillness that leads to the action.**

In a wonderful TED Talk, Barbara Oakley, a professor of engineering and author of *Learning How to Learn*, explained how we learn things that are hard to learn or very different from what we already know.[2] She should know. She flunked her way through math and science and didn't begin to explore engineering as a career until she was in her late twenties, after years as a specialist in Russian and Slavic languages. In her talk, she described two modes of thinking: focus mode and diffuse mode. Focus mode is exactly what it sounds like. It's how we think when we're trying to accomplish a task or memorize something. Our thinking is usually confined to neural paths we've already created. Diffuse mode is a more "relaxed set of neural states" that allows our thinking to take off, range widely, and process or even create new ideas. When we are learning, we need both. And when we feel stuck in our thinking, unable to understand a concept, unable to unravel a challenge, we especially need the diffuse mode.

How do we get there? We give our minds a break. We let them wander and jump from idea to idea and thought to thought until, eventually, the connection is made and we have a breakthrough. This is the practical power of time to reflect. I discovered all sorts of useful ideas in life and work as I relaxed my mind and let the sermon I was hearing lead me in new and interesting directions.

James Gorman, chairman and CEO of Morgan Stanley, told me that in life, we're always going to be dealing with the next thing that could make us lose perspective or distract us from seeing what's important. "It's like standing at the ocean and you're watching the waves come in. And you want them to stop for a little bit, but they just don't stop. . . . Somehow, you have to remove yourself from standing on the shoreline and find a quiet place under a quiet tree and give your mind time to reflect and to think."

For James, that space is created when he gets outside and exercises. For me, it's similar. Every house we've ever bought has had a huge, majestic tree in the yard or an awe-inspiring view. There's nothing like nature to inspire you to reflect on the connectedness of everything, on something greater than your own self-importance, and on gratitude for everyday beauty.

I believe we learn and are inspired to keep learning when we take time to ponder life's great mysteries, to feel gratitude, and to consider our connection and responsibility to others. We can find inspiration for reflection and sharing—and the learning that comes from both—in so many places in life. Wherever you find the time or however you approach the practice or whatever offers you inspiration, make time in your life for deep reflection. You may be surprised by the world of ideas and insights you discover within your own thinking. And consider spending some of that time with others so you can share what you discover.

Learning to Reflect

- If you had to add up the minutes, how much time do you think you spend per week in deep reflection, letting your mind wander, or just noodling?

- Think of a time when you struggled with a problem, a challenge, or a complex idea, and when you stepped away from it and gave your mind time to wander, it suddenly became clear. Where in your life could you do that right now to discover something essential?

- Where do you turn for inspiration, moments of gratitude, and enlightenment?

Learn to be humble—and confident

Chapter 14

Stay Right-Sized

Wendy, my wife, has a very delicate way of letting me know when I'm out of line. She gives me a loving kick to the psyche by saying, "You're not the CEO around here."

That fact was clear from the very beginning of our relationship.

When she and I first met in college, I thought she was the most beautiful girl on campus. I worshipped her from afar for three years, only confessing my feelings to friends. Finally, at the local pub one night during our senior year, she caught my probably unsubtle gaze and yelled down the length of the bar, "Hey, Novak, when are you going to have enough guts to ask me out?"

We were married less than a year later.

She is definitely my co-CEO. And without her, I never would have made it as far as I have in my career and life. She's *especially* good at keeping me right-sized—not letting my ego get too inflated and not letting my self-esteem get too deflated. For instance, when I was named CEO of the Year by *Chief Executive Magazine* in 2012, I was incredibly proud, because it's an honor bestowed by your peers (other CEOs vote from a list of nominees). I was invited to a dinner where I would give a speech. When we walked in, we were surrounded by photos of past honorees—Andy Grove of Intel, Herb Keller of Southwest

Airlines, Larry Bossidy of Honeywell, and so many more. Wendy scanned the photos of the business giants and said, "What the heck are *you* doing here?"

We both burst out laughing. "I'm asking myself the same question," I said.

It wasn't that Wendy didn't think I deserved some recognition. It was just an honest response to all the talent and prestige in the room, especially compared to where we had come from. That moment became the opening for my speech, and it brought the house down.

I've learned that the best leaders—*and* active learners—have an uncanny combination of confidence and humility. Confidence is important because nobody will follow you unless they believe you know where you're going and you'll find a way to get there. If that confidence isn't tempered by humility, though, it becomes arrogance. That's the gift that Wendy gives me. She boosts my confidence and delivers doses of humility as situations demand. And that has helped me continue to learn through personal ups and downs.

Humility is just the recognition that you can't do it by yourself— whatever "it" is—either because you simply can't, because you don't know enough, or because it won't be as fun or fulfilling if you go it alone. None of your big successes are yours alone, which is why active learners think in terms of "we" rather than "me." When you move through the world with this perspective, you open yourself to the ideas, opinions, and experiences of the people around you.

Confidence is simply the expectation that you'll find a way to win—somehow. That expectation comes with experience and learning, but the "somehow" almost always depends on a team, whether your colleagues, the people you lead, or your family and friends. I would argue that it's almost impossible to be truly confident *without* humility.

Together, the two give you a healthy dissatisfaction with the status quo that drives your desire to learn and grow. In *Above the Line*, Stephen Klemich and Mara Klemich, a leadership coach and a neuro-psychologist, write about four universal principles that explain why human beings do the things we do. Their model is based on deep psychological research and decades of testing and refinement. In it, *ego-driven* pride (you might call it arrogance) and *courageous* humility are opposites, and they have opposing goals. Ego-driven pride drives personal *promotion*, whereas courageous humility fosters personal *growth*. When we're strong in humility, we're "open to opportunities to learn from any person or experience. We're unafraid to try new things or new ways of accomplishing goals or to admit that we don't know or need help."[1] The other behaviors their research links to humility, especially being authentic and achievement oriented, are the types of behaviors we associate with *confidence*, showing that humility and confidence are two sides of the same coin.

As you advance in your career and accumulate experience and expertise, you will face a choice. As my friend and board director John Weinberg described it, you can either grow or swell. **People with swollen egos can't be active learners because they don't believe they have much to learn.** They think they have all the answers they need or the ability to come up with those answers all on their own. That kind of thinking doesn't breed true confidence; it breeds fear—because it's all on you.

Brian Cornell, Target CEO, would look for humility through a pronoun flip in his teams. "I've always believed that the best things have happened in the businesses that I've been involved in when the pronouns change. . . . When I hear somebody say, 'Brian said we need to do this,' I just shake my head." Rather than taking it as a sign of his brilliance or how much people respect him, he sees it for what it is: a sign that other people don't feel ownership of the idea or the plan, don't feel empowered, and don't believe in it. "But when I hear that pronoun flip, and it becomes 'Here's what *we're* gonna do, and here's what *we* believe in, and here's *our* strategy, and here's *our* plan,' magical things happen." And great results start to materialize. There's evidence for this. Researchers have found that companies led by CEOs who used more "we" language in their letters to shareholders produced better return on assets.[2]

To maintain your humility long term, stay focused on the "we." **It's through the contributions of other people that you'll learn, grow, make it across the finish line.** Lauren Hobart, the CEO of Dick's Sporting Goods, seems to understand this innately. When we talked, she turned every discussion about her accomplishments back onto the team. When I asked her about the success of Dick's e-commerce platform, she said, "First of all, it wasn't just me. There's a whole army of people who have been building Dick's technology and e-commerce over many, many years . . . well before I got to Dick's." And when I asked her how ideas are generated at the company, she said, "We get a ton of inspiration and ideas from store managers. Ed [Stack, founder and chairman] and I and the entire leadership team are out in the stores more than at almost any company I know of. . . . We check the environment, how the store is doing generally, but most of all our goal is to hear from the stores what they think the opportunities are. Some of our absolute best ideas have come out of the stores."

The same has been true of all the work we've done through the Lift a Life Novak Family Foundation. We have a strong focus on the people we partner with, the people who lead our programs, and the people who are on the front line making things happen. For instance, Margaret Duffy has been the executive director of the Novak Leadership Institute at University of Missouri since we founded it in 2016. I've told her many times that the only reason we felt confident founding the institute is because we knew we had a leader who could pull it off. Her ideas for turning the "Taking People with You" curriculum I had developed and honed at Yum! into an accredited twelve-credit-hour leadership program for college students were invaluable. She created a special chancellor's program for freshmen (to help them become better leaders at the university). And she's developed important partnerships that offer students real-world professional experiences. Every time I meet with the university president, Mun Choi, about the institute, I let him know that the success of the program is largely hers.

There was a time in the business world when an all-knowing, "my way or the highway" attitude was seen as the path to success. It's an outdated idea that probably never worked. People like that almost always top out early, are a bit miserable, or make other people miserable. They are limited in what they can accomplish because they aren't effective learners.

When I was promoted to run the Frito-Lay account at the advertising agency, I was only twenty-nine years old. My bosses sent me to work with Jack Byrum, a legendary image coach who had worked with Johnny Carson and other celebrities, to learn how to present myself as more mature and confident. The biggest thing I learned from Jack was the opposite of that outdated view of leadership: "Don't look up. Don't look down. Always look straight ahead," he told me. What he meant was that you're no better and no worse than anyone else, no matter your position, your age, your experience. Byrum believed in projecting a powerful "main man/woman" image, but if your ego comes across as bigger than it ought to be, no one will see you as a credible leader. Today, when I meet with younger people, I love it when they look me straight in the eye and tell me what they want to say, rather than what they think I want to hear.

When it comes to humble *learning*, another vital habit to develop is saying, "I don't know," an idea I touched on when writing about how to learn from people who know more than you. Coach John Wooden talked about that habit all the time. For instance, when he recruited Kareem Abdul-Jabbar (then known as Lew Alcindor), he had never coached a seven-foot-tall player, who he described as an *extra* tall player. He recognized his gap and went to players who were extra tall, like Wilt Chamberlain, to find out how they had been coached. And he went to the coaches of these players to find out the best approaches. I was fortunate enough to meet Wooden because one of our franchisees and a good friend, Eddie Sheldrake, had played basketball for him. The morning I spent with him at his modest home was one of the most fascinating of my life. He seemed to effortlessly exude wisdom, yet he was incredibly humble and generous.

The willingness to say I don't know became an imperative for most of us in early 2020 with the onset of Covid-19. We had no idea what would happen next. We turned to health-care professionals for guidance. Just one problem: they didn't really know either. It was a new virus, and they were doing their best to make educated estimates about how it would behave. Leaders in health care were in an especially tough spot. Madeline Bell, CEO of the world-renowned Children's Hospital of Philadelphia, told me, "In times of crisis . . . we sometimes have to develop new muscles." And the new muscle she had to develop was getting comfortable saying "I don't know." She had always felt that as the CEO, she needed to have an answer for every situation. As Covid-19 spread, and the hospital faced a financial crisis, that wasn't possible.

In the middle of the chaos, the revelation that helped her lead was that people didn't need her to know; they just needed to understand that there was a process for getting to answers. Open communication and listening were her go-to tools, but even more important was pushing decision-making down to the leadership teams. These were talented people who were more in touch with what was happening in their departments and groups. They knew better than she did, and they needed to respond quickly during the crisis. Holding on to all of the decision-making power would have made the crisis worse. And only through her model of humility were they able to stay focused on being flexible, being open to ideas and possibilities, and learning.

Too many people start to smell their own perfume as they rise, but Nathan Smith avoids that ego trap. Every year I play in the National Senior-Junior Championship golf tournament in Florida. I'm the senior golfer and Nathan is my junior partner. He's a tremendous amateur who has played in four masters, won the US Mid-Amateur tournament four times, and is the captain for the 2025 American Walker Cup team (an amateur contest between the United States, Great Britain, and Ireland). He's obviously a significantly better and much more accomplished player than I am. But when we're playing and I hit a terrible shot, what he says to me is, "We're good, partner, we're good." He reassures me and lets me know that he has my back. He puts his ego aside and recognizes the power of us as a team.

It's been said by management gurus Tom Rath and John Maxwell. It's been said by pastor Rick Warren and actor Clint Eastwood. It was even said by the Ancient One to Marvel's Doctor Strange—and she called it "the simplest and most significant lesson of all."

It's not about you.

If you can learn that lesson, you can learn almost anything.

Learning to Be Humble—and Confident

- Think of something you accomplished recently. Who helped you make it happen? What were their contributions?

- Have you ever let your ego get in the way of a good idea or a learning opportunity? How did that feel? What was the result?

- What experience, situation, or person in your life keeps you grounded? Who tells you, "You're not the CEO around here"?

Chapter 15

Wipe Out "Not Invented Here"

Learn to celebrate others' ideas

I once worked for a leader who loved to claim ownership of others' ideas. "We could reduce costs by doing X, Y, and Z," someone would say. And he'd reply, "You know, on the drive in this morning I was thinking the very same thing." Or I'd walk into his office on Monday morning and say, "That campaign could be more effective if we did A, B, and C." And he'd say, "I was thinking the very same thing when I was golfing this weekend."

In fairness, I came to him with lots of ideas, so maybe some did overlap. But you know something is a problem when it becomes a running joke in the office. People on the team would be chatting in the break room about plans for the weekend or vacation and one of us would say, "You know, I was thinking the very same thing"—to many laughs.

I'm a believer in managing up (and down and sideways), and I decided this guy needed to hear the truth, because it was starting to affect morale and erode respect for him. I knew the habit was born from insecurity, so I started with some genuine recognition. "You're a fantastic leader," I told him, "and smart. There's no question that you should have the job you do." And then I said, "You can't be think-ing the same thing we're all thinking all the time. It's important to celebrate other people's ideas, so that they keep sharing them. I think if you do that, you'll get more innovation, and we'll have a more successful team."

It worked. He broke the habit and became a more effective leader, people loved working for him, and the jokes in the break room stopped.

Most good ideas are already out there, either in practice or in somebody's head. That's why I made the idea of *learn from* part one of this book. But if you want to encourage people to actively share ideas and insights with you, show them that you have an open mind and a heart willing to share credit, or even give it to them entirely. **Active learners *celebrate* other people's ideas. Because they do, more good ideas come their way, which accelerates their learning and expands their possibilities.**

At Yum! we built our culture on purposeful recognition: recognize and celebrate the behavior you want to promote, and you'll get more of it. One of the behaviors we wanted to promote was know-how sharing. In a massive global company like ours, good ideas crop up all over but may not spread everywhere. If we could find the best ideas and share them across the company, it would help every restaurant improve. Leaders who shared best practices earned higher bonuses, and we told the whole company about it. The KFC team in Australia generated more new product innovations than any other. It came up with boneless filets, chicken skewers, and the Variety Big Box Meal, all ideas that were widely implemented. Because we gave the team members credit, they kept innovating and sharing what they came up with. And that grew everybody's potential.

Just because people share a good idea doesn't mean that others will adopt it, though. Often, people will shoot down good ideas because they aren't *theirs*. They're "not invented here." We saw this often. Good ideas were met with "that might work for her, but it couldn't work for me" or "I know what I'm doing."

I wanted to wipe out "not invented here" and get people to ask instead, "If it worked for them, why *couldn't* it work for us?" So, we also paid higher bonuses to the teams that did a great job of adapting and implementing new ideas from other stores. With all this celebration of (and compensation for) good ideas and how they were implemented or improved, the practice of becoming a know-how builder spread and created huge positive effects for the company.

Even when we don't agree with somebody's idea as a whole, we can celebrate what we do agree with in part. Larry Senn, the culture mentor I've cited several times already, taught me the technique of "appreciate . . . even more effective": start by sharing what you appreciate about a person's idea—what you think will work or what's especially creative or helpful about it. By celebrating the good, you tone down the person's defensiveness and set the stage for a productive conversation about how to make an idea even more effective. When a member of the leadership team at Yum! presented a new idea, we went around the table and talked about what we appreciated first and then moved on to our thoughts for improving it. People like talking about their ideas, so keep the conversation focused there and present your thoughts as contributions.

By the time I was helping build the culture at Yum!, I had already had great role models in the practice of sharing credit. In the early nineties, when I was working at Pepsi-Cola, bottled water was the fastest-growing segment of the beverage business. Wayne Calloway, the chairman at the time, always asked, "When are we going to get into the water business?" It was unlikely we were going to discover some exotic, untapped mountain spring somewhere, so we were focused on acquiring an existing bottled water company. But one day, Wayne finally asked an incisive, beautiful question that changed everything: "Why can't we just use our own bottling plants and make our own water?" He helped us realize that consumers didn't care where the water came from; they just cared about the purity. Quickly, we worked out a way to purify the water we were already using at our Pepsi bottling plants and we created Aquafina, which became the number one bottled water in the United States.

Here's the key: it was Wayne Calloway's idea and Wayne Calloway's insistence that pushed us to the water business, but Wayne never asked for or received any credit for Aquafina. He let us have the glory. I learned from Wayne that success is a tangible asset that leaders use to make others feel good about themselves and help the whole organization learn and grow. **Leaders should be accountable for what goes wrong and give away the credit for what goes right.** And the higher you rise in the organization, the more important it becomes to credit others, especially when you're the CEO and the public face of a company. People might put the losses on your shoulders, but they'll put the wins there, too. When we opened a childcare center at the Yum! restaurant support center, I received many accolades for my forward-thinking leadership. Truthfully, I was aware that it was happening and happy about it, but that was the extent of my involvement. The idea and its execution were the work of Anne Byerlein, our chief people officer, so I made sure to direct people, especially reporters, to her so they could focus on *her* forward-thinking leadership.

There will always be people, like that old boss of mine, who want to be credited as the source of good ideas and successful strategies. It can be easy to fall into the trap when you step into a new leadership role. You might want to focus on everything the previous leader didn't do well. You can use Steve Kerr's model to avoid that trap. When Steve took over as coach of the Golden State Warriors from Mark Jackson, who hadn't been able to deliver an NBA championship, he did *not* focus on what Jackson failed to do or why he felt Jackson fell short. He instead took every chance he could to credit Jackson for building a strong team that was ready to dominate. In his first year, Kerr led the Warriors to the championship, their first in forty years—and he gave much of the credit to Jackson. When I asked him about his team's league-leading and historically great passing game, he of course led with, "Well, I inherited an excellent passing team."

I'll admit that one of my professional regrets is that I was critical of a previous leader or too focused on the weaknesses of the team or ideas that failed. When I became president of KFC, I was too judgmental of the prior regime's inability to drive sales and work with the franchisees, for example. But their efforts made what I did next easier to accomplish and more successful, even if it was learning from what they had tried that hadn't worked.

When Frank Blake became the CEO of Home Depot in 2007, he followed Steve Kerr's example rather than mine. The board had to convince him to take the job because he didn't believe he was qualified. He was a lawyer by trade without any merchandising or retail experience. One of the first calls he made when he accepted the role was to his son, who happened to be a Home Depot store manager. He shared the news, and his son laughed. He thought Frank was joking. Frank convinced him he wasn't kidding, and then explained his first challenge. He had to record a video message that would be played in the break room of every store, reaching 350,000 associates, and he wasn't sure what he should talk about. Home Depot had not been performing well, and morale was low. What was the right message to send?

His son laughed again, said, "Good luck, Dad," and then paused before sharing a bit of brilliance. "I can tell you how I start each of my meetings. I read from *Built from Scratch*"—an insightful book by Bernie Marcus and Arthur Blank, Home Depot's founders, about how they built and grew the company. In every meeting, Frank's son celebrated ideas and foundational principles that had made the company successful from the start.

Now, other CEOs might have wanted to emphasize how they would put their own stamp on things, what they would change, how they would solve problems past leaders hadn't. But in his first message to associates, Frank talked about the inverted pyramid, a core idea in the founders' book. At the top, at the widest point, were customers. Then associates, then field support, then corporate support. At the bottom, in the tiny triangle that was left, the CEO. He sent a very clear message that the people who mattered most, and whose ideas and behaviors mattered most, were customers and associates. And from that day on, he found ways to celebrate them, which helped him successfully lead Home Depot through a difficult period (the Great Recession began a year after he took the role).

While Frank Blake is one of the smartest people I know, I tell people all the time that you don't have to be all that smart to be a CEO. You just have to be smart enough to recognize good ideas from smart people.

I've applied lessons I've learned from Frank as we've set up our family foundation. When I asked Ashley Butler, my daughter, to take on the role of executive director, I wanted her to find her own path forward, find her own identity as its leader, and feel confident in her abilities and choices. I wanted my confidence in her ideas and abilities to shine through in anybody who interacted with the foundation. The only way to do that was to make sure I wasn't casting a long shadow. I had to celebrate her ideas and not override them with my own whenever possible. By checking my ego and enthusiasm, I've made space for her to do amazing things. I celebrate her ideas in big ways, of course, but also subtly. When people want to talk to me about the foundation, I immediately make the conversation about Ashley or direct them to her. Now, people realize that she's the one they should go to first because she's the driving force behind our work in early childhood education, the Dare to Care Food Bank in Louisville, and the Wendy Novak Diabetes Institute.

Remember, people walk through life with all sorts of brilliant ideas stuck in their heads. Listening and asking better questions are important, but if we give people credit and celebrate their ideas, we encourage them to keep innovating and sharing—and then we all learn more together. Credit is essential to collaboration.

Learning to Celebrate Others' Ideas

- Do you ever feel like the people around you are holding back their best ideas? If so, why do you think that might be?

- Do you always give others the right amount of credit for their ideas and contributions? How do you do it?

- Whose idea or contribution could you celebrate today? What difference could it make in how they feel and how they behave?

Chapter 16

Round Up
on People

I'm a Theory Y leader all the way.

Back in 1960, Douglas McGregor, a management professor at MIT, described two leadership outlooks on human behavior in his book *The Human Side of Enterprise*. Those who fell into the Theory X category believed that employees had to be coerced, controlled, and threatened to do good work or take responsibility. Those who fell into Theory Y believed that people were generally creative, ingenious, and ready to take on responsibility, if they were treated accordingly.

I believe in running an organization based on the assumption that 99.9 percent of people want to do good, not bad or even mediocre, work. I trust in their positive intentions.

Active learners understand the power of trust and leverage it to learn more, faster. Trusting in positive intentions helps us overcome our natural defensiveness and listen with an open mind. It helps us overcome our bias against ideas from people we may not see as on our side—which is often just a story we've made up about them. When we move beyond that kind of thinking, we're more collaborative and we get to better action faster.

But that kind of trust doesn't always come naturally. We're too much on alert for threats in our environment. We're too ready to interpret people's actions through a negative lens, especially when there's a long-standing issue or conflict. I don't want you to think I'm naive, and I don't mean to sound like a Pollyanna. My biggest disappointments in life haven't been in business results or ideas that flopped—they've been in people who have betrayed my trust. But I *know* that it's still worth starting from a position of trust.

In 1994, Wayne Calloway, chairman of PepsiCo, asked me if I would want to be president of KFC (I was COO of Pepsi-Cola, the beverage division, at the time). I pretended that I needed some time to talk it over with my family, but I knew I'd say yes. And I knew Wendy would support me in that decision. I couldn't wait to get started.

When I accepted the job, I got more calls offering condolences than congratulations. Wayne asked me to take the job because I had built a reputation for helping to turn around struggling businesses— and KFC had been struggling under PepsiCo's ownership. It never achieved its business plan and had had no same-store sales growth for *seven straight years*. It had become a graveyard for PepsiCo executives. To franchisees, who owned 70 percent of the KFC restaurants, corporate was seen as a bunch of outsiders who didn't enjoy fried chicken and didn't believe KFC could beat our competitors. They also held a majority of the marketing votes, which meant they controlled everything from advertising to new products, and they often voted as a bloc—against us. Trust was so frayed at the time that the franchisees were suing us over territorial rights.

I had inherited a business in decline and a broken franchise system waging open warfare with us.

I started at KFC on a Monday. We had a conference with the best franchisees in the system scheduled for that Wednesday. The department heads were urging me to cancel it. "Oh, no," I said. "I can't wait to meet these people." Even if all I accomplished was telling them I was looking forward to working with them, I was *going* to have that meeting.

On that Wednesday, one of the first things I said was, "I want you to know one thing: I love Kentucky Fried Chicken"—because that's true. Then I said, "Look, I don't know this business, but I'm going to go through the process of learning it. I'm going to find out what the front lines are thinking, and I'm going to listen to our customers. Then I'm going to go out to share what I've learned with you. And then I'm going to ask you how to fix what's not working. Together we're going to develop a plan to turn this business around."

This was a tough bunch, and I knew that no matter what I said, they were focused on the contract problem. So I added, "I know there's a contract issue, but we can't fix this business by fighting each other. If we can't work together, there isn't going to be any business left to fight over anyway. I'm not going to even talk about the contract until we fix this business, so don't even bring it up."

We started turning the business around in less than a year, in large part because we extended our trust first. We rounded up rather than down, assuming franchisees were more than their most biting remarks or their most aggressive actions. And that helped them return the trust. **In any relationship, business or personal, somebody has to trust more or trust first to break inertia and build up positive momentum.**

The strategy I used and that you can use when you're finding it hard to overcome your cynicism or shift your attitude is to *focus on shared goals*. When you spend more time thinking about how you and another person or group are alike rather than how you're different, you can work around the natural tendency to consider other groups a threat.

I began shifting the attitude of everybody who worked in corporate by "shocking the system," which means taking whatever the conventional wisdom or prevailing attitudes are and turning them on their ear. I announced to everyone in the building: "We've hated franchisees for so long it's killing us. From now on, we love franchisees. We absolutely adore them. We want to work with them, we want to learn from them, and we want them to feel the love. Why? Because we don't have a choice." I saw us as one big in-group, with a long list of shared goals, all of us depending on each other to succeed.

Besides, the franchisees are entrepreneurs. A lot of them started with nothing and worked to become multimillionaires owning well-run organizations that manage more than a hundred restaurants. We'd have been crazy not to listen to them, learn from them, rely on them. But first, we had to stop seeing them as the enemy. In spite of the voting bloc, and in spite of the lawsuit, we had to trust them and their intentions.

I had enough leadership experience at that point to understand the power of trust. Stephen M. R. Covey calls it "the speed of trust," also the title of his bestselling book, because when trust in an environment is high, everything moves faster. He told me he had this revelation early on as CEO of the Covey Leadership Center, the company founded by his father Stephen R. Covey. The company was working with two suppliers to produce a product. One was a high-trust partner, and all the work with them happened smoothly and quickly. The other was low trust, a relationship that required extra meetings, processes, and inspections. It was slow and costly. Stephen began to see the world through this lens of trust-as-speed. Eventually he validated it with research and it became the core of his company's programs on building trust.

Our situation with the franchisees was perfect anecdotal proof. Progress on important initiatives had been molasses slow, and that had to change. The finance people will say that new products turned KFC around. I always say it was a triumph of human spirit because we only began generating or discovering those ideas for new products once we started trusting each other enough to work together.

Take chicken tenders—which we originally called Crispy Strips. R&D couldn't figure out how to distribute them nationally, at a time when it seemed everyone had some kind of chicken tender product except us, the company known for doing chicken right. I'd been at KFC for about seven months when I learned that there was a franchisee in Arkansas selling Crispy Strips, and sales at his stores were up 9 percent.

Restaurant chains rely on familiarity and consistency. For a franchisee to develop their own product line is typically a huge no-no. In the old days, before we were focused on developing trust and collaboration, I guarantee the franchisee wouldn't have even told us what he was doing, and if we had found out about it on our own, we would have gone there and squashed him like a bug for changing products without permission.

Instead, I sent our marketing and R&D teams to see how he was doing it. He took them to his supplier, who showed them how we could deliver the same product nationally. That insight evolved into the most successful new product KFC had introduced since the Colonel's original recipe. *And* we sent the message to franchisees that we trusted their intentions, and they could trust in ours—that we just wanted to champion good, successful ideas. It was a brand-new day.

Shortly after that, we solved the contract issue. We gave the franchisees the one-and-a-half-mile exclusivity they wanted around each of their restaurants, and we got the right to hire and fire our advertising agency, which gave us more marketing control. A near-decade-long dispute was solved fairly quickly because we had learned to trust.

Trust-building pays off big time, especially within teams or organizations. It creates environments of psychological safety, which according to Amy Edmondson, Harvard Business School professor and author of *The Fearless Organization*, are a blend of trust and respect. Her research has proven that **in companies that work to eliminate fear, people are far more likely to speak up, share ideas, be truth-tellers, be innovators, and learn from each other.** They give their best individual effort for the benefit of the whole.

Brad Richards, two-time Stanley Cup winner (with the Tampa Bay Lightning and Chicago Blackhawks) and a playoff MVP, talked about how crucial this was to his teams' ability to succeed in the high-pressure, bright-lights playoff games. Sometimes, the first-tier hockey line, the team's top players, aren't clicking on the ice. In those moments, a coach will substitute in players from the second line or even the third. For those players, this can be a big deal. They don't always get playing time in big games. On less safe teams, those moments can lead to resentment or jealousy. The first-line players don't want to share the spotlight, don't want to be outdone by others on their team, and the second-line players let their desire to shine in the moment drive them on the ice, which doesn't create good team play. On successful teams, everybody trusts that every player is there to do what's best for the team. They all believe in putting together the best line in the moment to win. They trust in each other's positive intentions, so they can offer authentic support and encouragement. And together, they win.

My podcast has been built on trust and safety. Most of my guests are CEOs of large public companies, and some almost never agree to interviews. Mine was the first podcast that Dave Calhoun, the CEO of Boeing, had ever done. He had been hired as CEO to lead the company through the crisis it faced after two of its 737s crashed, killing 346 people. The company was under investigation, its culture was in trouble, and he had a lot of work to do to turn the company around. But he came on the show because he trusts me. Guests know I'm not going to trick them into saying the wrong thing or use some kind of bait-and-switch interview tactic. That said, I'll be fair and ask them about tough situations, because those are some of the most important learning moments they can share with listeners. But trust and safety allow people to be vulnerable, and that's what makes our conversations so powerful.

As important as it is for us to trust in positive intentions, if we want people to trust in ours, we need to behave accordingly. We need to build a well of trust to draw on, and as Stephen Covey explains, an important factor in that is our integrity.

For example, when we had the vision for the Novak Leadership Institute at the University of Missouri, and committed to funding it with a massive donation, the school committed to a permanent, dedicated building—a new welcome center to be called the Novak Leadership Institute. We felt this new building would give the institute even more legitimacy, showcase the university's dedication to leadership education, and attract students by leveraging it as a competitive advantage.

Years after this commitment, that building still doesn't exist. Covid-19, rising construction costs, and supply chain issues have conspired to halt progress. I could get angry about the lack of follow-through on a commitment. I could stamp my feet and make threats. Or I could be guided by the work that *is* happening, the incredible leadership of Margaret Duffy, other forms of support from the university, and trust that, eventually, it will happen. The leaders at the University have built a well of trust to draw on, so I feel confident that as we work toward that goal, we'll keep collaborating and learning new ways to make the institute everything we want it to be.

When somebody makes a mistake or fails to follow through on a commitment, our trust is tested. But **we have the phrase *honest mistake* for a reason. Assuming negative intent cuts us off from possibility and positive experiences.** Eric Church, the award-winning country singer–songwriter, experienced that in a big, stadium-sized way. He starts every show by lowering a huge flag, as wide as the stage, representing whatever state or country he's in. One night, when he was visiting me, he told the story of the show in Texas where, somehow, the Texas flag had been hung upside down.

All of a sudden, the crowd began booing and chanting insults, and he didn't know why. When he realized what had happened, he immediately apologized and told them he would get it fixed and make it up to them.

We talked about the reaction of the crowd. I wondered out loud what percentage of the people assumed that somebody had made an honest mistake? And what percentage took that mistake personally and went on the offensive against a performer they had paid good money to see? Honestly, why would Eric and his crew possibly want to alienate tens of thousands of his fans?

We're all human; we're all going to lose our tempers or handle a delicate situation poorly or not show as much compassion as we should or make a poor judgment call. When we're on the receiving end, if we can take a breath, find a little empathy, and trust that the other person has good intentions that didn't pan out, we can avoid a total breakdown in the flow of ideas and learning and collaboration.

. . .

I read a striking definition of trust recently: "Trust is a relationship of reliance."[1] Aren't we all reliant on each other if we want to learn, grow, and expand our possibilities? We can choose to support that relationship or tear it down. If we choose the second option, we're only limiting ourselves. If we choose the first, the possibilities are infinite.

Learning to Trust in Positive Intentions

- Are you naturally a Theory X or a Theory Y leader? If you're Theory X and you don't trust that your employees want to do good work without being coerced, what's one piece of proof from your team or company that would convince you otherwise?

- Have you ever discounted an idea because you didn't trust the person it came from and then later discovered it was a great idea? Was your lack of trust valid?

- Where in your life right now is a trust issue slowing down your learning or growth? Could you extend trust first? How?

Part Three

LEARN BY

Experience is the
teacher of all things.

—Julius Caesar

Learn by
pursuing joy

Chapter 17

Blockers
and Builders

In my early forties, I faced a tough decision. It was 1997, three years into my role as president of KFC, and together with the franchisees, we had turned the company around. PepsiCo chairman Roger Enrico told me that he would like me to take on the role of president of Frito-Lay, the snack food division.

It was an amazing opportunity to lead a bigger and more prestigious division in the company. (PepsiCo had three core divisions—beverages, snack foods, and restaurants.) I had already held leadership positions in the other two divisions, and spending time in the third was a logical step toward taking on the biggest jobs in the corporation.

But I turned it down. It was absolutely the best decision I ever made.

I had learned something important about myself. I absolutely *loved* working in restaurants. I love food, especially the process of creating new recipes and new products that I can envision people enjoying with their families. I love the marketing process for restaurants and the immediate feedback on campaigns. And I loved the people, the frontline employees, and the customers, who always made me think of my parents.

Understanding this about myself allowed me to pursue what brought me joy rather than blindly follow the expected path—something

I have done many times throughout my career. By pursuing my joy builders (which shifted over time), I was engaged, energized, and interested in what I was doing. I learned more because I *wanted* to learn more. And all that learning boosted my opportunities. Not long after I turned down the role with Frito-Lay, PepsiCo announced a plan to spin off the restaurants into a new public company. My decision to stay in restaurants brought me to my role as CEO of Yum! Brands, the greatest job I could imagine, and one I would be privileged to hold for seventeen years.

Active learners know that we learn better when we're feeling more positive emotions. In the article "The Neuroscience of Joyful Education," neurologist, teacher, and author Judy Willis breaks down the essentials of the research that backs this idea: "The truth is that when we scrub joy and comfort from the classroom, we distance our students from effective information processing and long-term memory storage."[1] When we feel engaged and motivated, and find pleasure in the learning process, we get hits of positive neurochemicals like dopamine and serotonin. They help information flow more freely through the brain and boost our memory. We learn more, we make better connections (pattern thinking), what we learn sticks in our memories better, and we have more breakthroughs.

This is the first chapter in part three, on learn by doing, and the best place to start is to learn by doing what brings you joy. When you start there, all other learning becomes easier.

Alberto Carvalho, once the superintendent of the Miami-Dade public school system and now the superintendent of the Los Angeles public school system, told me, "I've never met anyone who was terrifically successful at something they did not excel at and that they did not love. Expertise and passion are unbeatable." His own deep love for learning and his passion for the power of education to transform lives helped him turn the Miami-Dade district around. It helped him make things happen politically and in the community, especially for some of the most vulnerable students and their families.

Alberto would not have been as effective if his work hadn't brought him so much joy. The district would not have gone on such a powerful learning journey under his leadership.

Ed Herlihy told me that joy in your work also builds your tenacity and work ethic—both of which boost learning. The more committed you are, the more willing you are to invest in learning even the hardest things. Ed should know. He's a legendary mergers and acquisitions lawyer, representing companies involved in takeover battles or organizations on the brink of collapse. And in 2008, Hank Paulson, US secretary of the treasury, asked Ed to help the treasury figure out what to do about the housing and financial crisis. Ed helped orchestrate the hostile takeover—the largest *ever*—of the two financial giants Fannie Mae and Freddie Mac by the US government. (They were put into conservatorship.) "We had to restructure very complex financial arrangements," Ed told me. "And that began a period of six months where I worked 24/7. I never had a day off or a break." During those six months, Ed went from helping the treasury to representing Bank of America in buying Merrill Lynch. Then he helped Morgan Stanley become a bank holding company. And then he helped Wells Fargo break up the Citigroup deal with Wachovia so that it could acquire Wachovia. "It took me six months to work on [these deals] and six months to recover."

"In what we do, either you're in the game or you're not," he said. When we spoke, he was still on call, twenty-four hours a day, and had been for eight months, as part of a complex deal that, of course, he couldn't tell me about. But those endless hours of intense learning and action fly by for him. "I love the firm. I'm passionate about the work. . . . It's something that still really stimulates me."

Joy is our source of purpose, passion, mission—and the most enjoyable path to learning.

Of course, pursuing your joy requires that you know where to find it in your life and work. Not many people consider what makes them happiest, beyond things that aren't necessarily within their control. When I wrote *Take Charge of You* with sports performance coach

Jason Goldsmith, we tackled this question at the start. If you're going to coach yourself to success, you need to know what you're coaching yourself *toward*. We suggested people start by mining their experiences for **joy blockers** (we're a bit better at remembering negatives) and then shift and search for their **joy builders.**

Try asking yourself this: What's getting in the way of my joy? If you're not sure, think back to some of your worst days, or a job that frustrated you or made you miserable or unfulfilled. *What* made it so difficult for you? Be as specific as possible. Did you want to be in a different role? Was there one specific thing you were required to do that you dreaded doing? Was there a kind of person or team you had to work with that brought you down?

I'm sure you can think of examples. We all hate our jobs sometimes. Even if you *can* think of examples, though, you may never have deeply reflected on or logically analyzed *why* you were unhappy in a particular situation or environment.

I wish I could give a good example of this kind of reflection from my own life, but I've rarely felt that way. And I don't think most active learners have much experience with it either, at least not for long. **When active learners find themselves in a situation that's too full of their joy blockers, they learn their way out of it or they learn their way around the blockers fast. They know if they don't, they'll stagnate.** They also know that just because a job or situation doesn't come preloaded with joy builders doesn't mean it's *the wrong choice.* It just means it's up to them to find a way around the blockers.

Here's what that looks like in action. About seven years before I turned down the job with Frito-Lay, I moved from head of marketing of Pizza Hut, a job I loved, to take on the role of executive vice president of marketing and sales for the beverage division, Pepsi-Cola. I was excited by the opportunity, but also had doubts. The previous four people in the position had all been canned or moved quickly to another job—it was a real up-or-out possibility. I should have seen the signs of things to come when I picked up the *Wall Street Journal* on my first day and read the headline, "*Wojak* Named Head of Pepsi

Marketing." (I wasn't nearly as upset that it got my name wrong as my mom and dad were.)

At the start, everything felt a bit off the mark. At Pizza Hut, I had fun generating new, exciting ideas with an enthusiastic team, and we made great things happen. But at Pepsi, the culture was entrenched, the working environment was aloof, and the marketing and advertising plans "established." My efforts to inject fun and excitement into the environment or into our ideas didn't play well. Pepsi was also more hierarchical than Pizza Hut, and the higher up you got, the less you were supposed to do. Every day, I heard, "We'll take care of that for you." I didn't want that.

It threw me off my game for the first few months, the only time in my career when I didn't look forward to coming to work every morning. But I knew if I persevered, I'd find a way to make the position work for me. I just had to find a way around my joy blockers and start getting things done my way.

The right opportunity showed up with Mountain Dew. I thought the brand had more potential than we realized. At the time, the well-established marketing guidelines for Mountain Dew required soothing water imagery—mountain lakes, running streams. It was "rural" and "outdoorsy." I wanted to build a new image, a task I relished taking on wherever I worked because it was creative and collaborative. I wanted to take Mountain Dew out of the country and into the city, making it more mainstream. But I couldn't get Alan Pottasch, the legendary head of Pepsi advertising and the father of "the Pepsi Generation," to buy in.

So, I circumvented the system and approached another legend, Phil Dusenberry, the head of the BBDO advertising agency, to create a campaign for *Diet* Mountain Dew, because nobody was paying much attention to it.

Phil and his team created a campaign that featured "the Dew Boys" whose tagline was "Been there, done that." People picked up on the phrase right away. (Creating an expression that becomes part of the vernacular is every marketer's dream, and I still smile today when I hear someone say it.) Diet Mountain Dew became our fastest-growing beverage, so we extended the effort to regular Mountain Dew with the edgier and more energetic "Do the Dew" campaign, centered on extreme sports. It was *very* successful. By focusing on my joy builders and working around my joy blockers, I was back on my game.

What are your joy builders? And how can you pursue them? Think about some of your *best* days or jobs—times when you felt especially purposeful, powerful, optimistic, and joyful. What was happening? What were you doing? Who were you doing it with? What specific things made you feel happy, excited, or energized? Try looking at your joy blocker examples and asking, What would have made me happier in those situations?

Sometimes, finding your joy in a role or in life is about the smaller things that roll up into the bigger things. Jesse Cole, owner of the Savannah Bananas exhibition baseball team, told me that he was challenged early on in his career. His focus was all about making the next career move—becoming a general manager, a partner, an owner. He was impatient, and at the same time, the progress he was making wasn't bringing him much happiness. Some soul searching led to a realization: "My greatest happiness is seeing other people have the time of their life, having fun, loving what they do," he told me. "When I can share, teach, and have fun with others, it brings me more joy, more success, more gratitude." And that's what he set out to do.

The Savannah Bananas are like the Harlem Globe Trotters of baseball. They put on a show for the fans and let the fans help create it. Parking attendants dress in banana costumes. Tickets are scratch-n-sniff. A marching band welcomes fans into the stadium. The first-base coach break dances between plays. The team performs skits between innings. And Jesse is usually there in his signature bright-yellow tuxedo and top hat, leading cheers in the stands. They will do anything to make sure fans are having fun.

All that joy generates a lot of success. They sell every ticket every season and have a massive waiting list.

Jesse writes a thank-you letter every day to somebody who made an impact in his life or business. He sent me a thank-you letter describing what he learned from my books and how he used it. I was so moved and intrigued, I just had to talk to him. He told me he had already written more than a thousand such thank-you letters. Later, when he accepted my invitation to be on my podcast, he said, "That gives me joy, that gives me happiness . . . but it's also spreading gratitude to someone else."

Pursuing joy helps you spread joy, which creates a kind of virtuous cycle of learning.

When I pursue work that brings me joy, I develop contagious enthusiasm, which helps me attract talented people to my mission, which helps me learn more and faster. That was certainly true when I was hired to lead marketing at Pizza Hut in 1986, when the company had hit a slump. We needed good ideas, great collaboration, and top talent. We were also headquartered in Wichita, Kansas, though, which isn't considered one of the world's business meccas. But people will go anywhere if they feel they can be part of an exciting growth story. I put together what I would argue was one of the best in the business. We recruited people from General Mills and Procter & Gamble and brought in talent from big cities. Nearly everyone who worked in that department went on to become a superstar. I think I can say without much ego that my enthusiasm was part of their decision to join. If people think they'll have a chance to grow, opportunities to pursue their own joy builders, and a positive environment, they'll come.

We created the iconic "Makin' it great" advertising campaign, which became our rallying cry. We introduced successful specialty pizzas—Meat Lover's, Cheese Lover's, Pepperoni Lover's. We created kids' nights, offering a free personal pan pizza and mini party kits. We did tie-ins with movies, the NCAA basketball tournament, and more. We loved the work we were doing and the environment we were doing it in. Suddenly, we saw weekend customer volumes on Tuesday nights. We were constantly breaking sales records.

The importance of loving what you do is one of the oldest clichés for a good reason. It's essential to getting ahead. If you don't like what you're doing now, you need to keep looking. My sister Susan decided in her late forties that she was burned out in her job as division controller for a nursing-home company. She dreamed of owning her own clothing boutique, so one day she got up the courage to quit her job and follow her passion. She opened her own store, called Sisters, and couldn't wait to go to work every day. The business had its challenges, but Susan was happier than ever. Happy in challenge is better than miserable in success. Her only regret was that she didn't do it sooner. Life's too short not to do what you love, not to pursue joy, if you get the chance.

Once you find your joy, do what it takes to hold onto it. Jim Nantz, the Emmy Award–winning sports commentator, the voice of the NFL on CBS, the NCAA's March Madness, and the PGA's Masters Tournament. In the 1990s, ABC had an open spot on *Good Morning America*, and Roone Arledge, head of ABC Sports, wanted Jim to take it. Arledge called Nantz daily. Jim was trying to hold him off to give himself time to think about the opportunity. He told Roone he would be home from a work trip to Italy in a week but had to immediately fly to LA for his next gig. "Could we do it the next week?" Jim asked.

Jim returned from Italy, switched out his luggage, slept a few hours, and then headed to the airport. When he boarded the plane, he found Roone Arledge in the seat next to his! For six hours, Roone recruited Jim for the job. More money, a less frenetic travel schedule, and other perks. Jim was honored, of course. But in the end, he had to turn it down. "It wasn't in my heart," he told me. He loved sports, he knew what his joy builders were, and he had already found the job that kept him connected to that joy.

If you want to maximize what you can learn in a week, a month, or a year, pursue what brings you joy. Learn by learning about *you* and then take action based on what you discover. You'll be amazed by how far you go.

Learning by Pursuing Joy

- Have you ever analyzed your joy builders? If not, take the time to do it now. What are the things you've loved doing across different jobs, roles, or aspects of your life? Dig into the nuances— those specific core factors that make all the difference.

- What's something you've pursued or learned about all on your own, without much external motivation, because you were passionate about it? Did you find the learning process to be easier?

- Do you currently love what you do? If not, is there a way to pursue your joy builders within the role? What could that look like?

Chapter 18

Everyone Else Is Taken

Learn by being yourself—your best self

Back in the nineties, as I was moving up the ranks in PepsiCo, Montblanc fountain pens were a status symbol for leaders, like a badge in the breast pocket of executives. I got one to feel part of the club, especially because I didn't have some of the other badges my colleagues had, like an MBA or an Ivy League education. A few weeks later, I tucked it into my shirt pocket without the cap on. Black ink spread out into a giant stain, ruining my shirt. I hurled the pen across the room in anger and broke it.

I never bought another. I took that moment as a sign, a reminder that I wasn't a fountain pen kind of guy. It just wasn't me.

You may know the quote often attributed to Oscar Wilde: "Be yourself; everyone else is taken." (What he actually wrote is more cynical: "Most people are other people. Their thoughts are someone else's opinions, their lives a mimicry, their passions a quotation."[1]) Maybe because of my background and the potential prejudgments that came with it, I've spent most of my life working hard to just be me—to understand who that person is, the contributions I have to offer, what I believe, and my purpose and passions. If I hadn't followed this path, I would have missed out on so much learning.

Active learners know that it's hard to learn when your mental energy is focused on trying to be somebody other than yourself. Instead of being open and curious, you'll be defensive. You'll be putting up barriers and withholding your brilliance. And then the people around you will do the same. Most of us can sense when people aren't being authentic, and it makes us trust them less.

Marvin Ellison, chairman, president, and CEO of Lowe's, was one of very few Black leaders there in the 1990s. "There was virtually no diversity at the corporate office," he told me. "There's no one that looks like me. There are very few people who have spent most of their career in the field. And there's nobody from the South. So, I'm looking around, and I believe and feel like I am the only person in that entire corporate environment that looks, that thinks, or has a background like me."

A few months in, his wife asked him how it was going, because he seemed stressed. The job wasn't that hard, he told her. He knew what he was doing, but he didn't feel like he fit in or that he could succeed in that culture. "She looked at me and said, 'Just try being yourself. Just relax, just be yourself, and see how that works out.'" Her advice made Marvin remember the words of his dad: "We may not have the nicest car, we may not live in a nice house, you may not wear the nicest clothes every day. But always remember, no one can beat you at being you. So, whenever you feel as though you're not achieving the thing that you believe you deserve, just focus on being the best you that you can be."

It was an aha moment for Marvin. **"I realized that by fitting in, I was actually working two jobs. I was working the job I was being paid to do. And then I was working a job being someone that I wasn't. I was doing double duty while everyone else was doing single duty."** He changed his approach. He dressed in a style that was professional, but more aligned with his personality, cultural background, and preferences rather than trying to blend in with everybody else. That was just surface, though. The important changes were in what and how he communicated.

When I sat in a meeting, if there was something that I felt didn't support the field, I would raise that point, but I'd raise it with facts, and I would raise it in a constructive way. And then I thought, I'm the only Black person up here. Let me provide some diversity of perspective to ensure we're making the right decisions for this consumer group. I would share thoughts, anecdotes, ideas about the Black community and ways we could be more effective.

Before I knew it, people were gravitating toward me. They wanted to know what I thought. They were inviting me to be part of project groups and focus groups because I no longer showed up as a commodity. . . . [They were] interested in what I had to say because it was unique, it was refreshing, and it was scarce. I learned that as a Black man in corporate America, as a Black executive operating in a world where I don't have a lot of people that look like me, the best thing I can do is be the best possible, most authentic me that I can be—in a way that's progressive, in a way that is educational, that helps make the organization better by bringing my unique learnings, my unique life, and my unique perspective to the conversation.

Active learners like Marvin pursue authenticity by recognizing their unique value and talents, figuring out what matters to them and why, and then leveraging it to have a positive impact.
Many studies have shown how this sense of self-worth can impact our ability to learn. Researchers have found that kids with good self-esteem, social and emotional awareness, and an understanding of their strengths do better in the classroom. I've seen the profound effects through our work with Global Game Changers, which offers a completely free elementary school curriculum for social-emotional learning. Cofounder Jan Helson's background is in food manufacturing. When we asked her about the inspiration for the organization, she told us how she would watch people on the floor of the manufacturing facility get constructive criticism from a foreman, go to lunch, and never come back. Their

self-esteem was so low that even pointing out a mistake or offering some coaching was a blow they couldn't take. She recognized that many people who worked those jobs may not have had opportunities to develop strong self-esteem growing up. By the time they became employees of her company, they were missing the tools they needed to receive criticism and *learn*. She teamed up with her daughter, Rachel, to answer the question, How can we grow self-esteem, empathy, and a service mindset as early as possible in life?

Their model is based on strengths-based learning and the benefits to our own well-being of having an "others" focus. For young kids, they simplified this beautifully: "my talent + my heart = my superpower." The curriculum teaches kids early to be their best selves, because that's the path to making a difference—and that's what *active* learners are all about. They understand that the best way to have a positive impact on circumstances and people is to bring their whole, wonderful self to a situation. When my daughter, Ashley Butler, head of the Lift a Life Novak Family Foundation, learned about the program, she couldn't wait to tell me about it. We immediately decided our foundation would help fund it. The work the organization has done in schools, especially in struggling communities, has been transformative.

Generally we all *want* to be ourselves; it makes us happier, we contribute more, and we learn and grow faster. But that doesn't mean it's easy. Our "comparison culture," especially in broadcast and social media, makes it more and more difficult to fight the message that we should try to be more like other people.

Bill Rhodes, CEO of Auto Zone, was lucky to have been raised hearing an opposite message. "My parents taught me, 'No idols,'" he told me. "You're never going to be the best athlete, you're never going to be the most handsome, but just go be the best *you* that you can be. And so, I spend every day saying, 'I don't want to be anybody else.'"

The other big hurdle is dysfunctional corporate cultures that send a message that only certain people bring value. A PwC survey of more than 52,000 people showed that one of the top factors for people who were considering leaving their jobs was whether they felt they could be themselves at work—66 percent said it was extremely or very important to feel they could.[2] As a leader, I fought to break down the hurdle that culture can create every chance I got. **I knew we couldn't succeed if we weren't all learning from each other, and that could only happen if everybody's unique perspective and talents were in the mix.**

I had my first real test in breaking down these barriers when I became president of KFC in 1994. I split my time between Connecticut and Louisville, Kentucky, home of KFC's headquarters, so that Wendy could finish her master's degree and Ashley could finish out her school year. On my first flight down, I felt both excited and daunted. I had wanted to be "president of something" for a long time, so you would think I had had plenty of time to figure out the *kind* of president I wanted to be. But I hadn't. The immensity of my new job hit me. The decisions I made, the actions I took, and how I showed up every day would impact the lives of 100,000 team members. I spent that plane ride in deep reflection.

PepsiCo was essentially the university where I received my MBA, with plenty of brilliant professors to learn from. And despite its best efforts to be otherwise, PepsiCo had always been primarily a top-down company. Among the upper management, there was a tendency to maintain emotional distance that put barriers between you and the people who worked for you.

That just wasn't me. I had always been a bit of an odd duck—the one among the Brooks Brothers power suits with his shirttail sticking out and a Montblanc pen leaking all over his shirt. Now that I was the one people would be looking to as a model for our culture, it was even more important to me that I come across as just a member of the team. I was the one who ultimately got to make the calls, but this wasn't going to be like PepsiCo. It couldn't be, because that wasn't me. And in realizing this, I was freed from trying to live up to some ideal, some *idol*, of what a president should be. That might seem like a small thing, but for me, it was a revelation, and it affected everything I did from then on.

I *really* like to win, but I operate on the idea that we can have fun and be positive while doing it—that being upbeat and making people feel good about their contributions is the best way to win. Because I understood this about myself, I made some changes right away that spawned a new corporate culture focused on recognition and people. I wanted us to take the business seriously but take ourselves a bit *less* seriously. I wanted to develop a relaxed, casual atmosphere that de-emphasized titles and hierarchy and encouraged everyone to work together, support each other, and have *fun*.

I started with our headquarters, which we renamed the "restaurant support center"—hardly a top-down approach. (We were the first company to use that kind of language for our headquarters.) This office was an antebellum-style mansion, built by the onetime president of KFC and later governor of Kentucky John Y. Brown to look like the White House. It was filled with expensive antiques and original paintings. I felt like I was working in a museum, and not a fun one, so I got rid of most of the antique furniture and replaced much of the artwork with pictures of our people, an idea I got when I visited Southwest Airlines. We created the Walk of Leaders, a hallway filled with a pictorial history of our brands and photos of people we recognized for great performance. I instituted the floppy rubber chicken recognition award, which I'll tell you more about in chapter 27. These changes helped shift the atmosphere, but they only worked because people could see that it was authentically my style. I brought my authentic self to work, so others did, too. It made a massive difference in our ability to turn the business around fast.

How can you get to that level of self-awareness and understanding? Everybody comes at it a bit differently, but you've already started if you're this far through the book. For instance, in chapter 1, I shared the idea of creating a timeline of your life and examining how it has shaped your values. In chapter 2, I wrote about analyzing the kind of environments you learn best in. And in the previous chapter, I shared the joy-builders exercise. If you've thought through these exercises and others, you've been building your self-awareness.

Once you have that foundation, **it's all about bringing who you are to the moment so that you're comfortable and open-minded enough to learn important lessons and ideas as they arise.** Pam Sherman, an executive leadership and communication coach and experienced actress, uses acting techniques to make this magic happen. She created an exercise called Rehearse "You." "Rehearsing sounds strange when we're talking about being authentic and truthful," Pam wrote. "But most of us have suppressed aspects of our selves for a long time. We need to practice bringing our full character to life so that we can feel comfortable and natural in the moment."[3] Try to imagine the kind of situation where you struggle to be authentic. Maybe it's when you need to share an opinion in a team meeting or speak in public (I had that problem for years) or have a tough conversation with someone—any situation that often makes you think, "Geez! I wish I had said or done . . ." When you've got one in mind, ask, What about the situation is making me hold back who I am? Then ask, If being me looks like X, Y, and Z (based on your values, your strengths, your purpose), how does that translate to this situation? What would my character say? What would my character do? What would my body language be? Finally, the next time you're in that situation, try to bring that "character" you've rehearsed to life.

Will Ahmed, the founder of WHOOP, a wearable health and fitness technology company, told me he turned to meditation to tackle the challenge of bringing himself to his role. He had reached a critical transition point in building the company. It had raised about $10 million and had built a team of fifteen or twenty people. It's a growth stage that can be tough for a lot of entrepreneurs. "I felt like I wasn't in control," Will told me. "I felt out of balance. I felt like things were coming out of my mouth, and then I was realizing I had said them." He told me he was in a constant state of reactiveness. "I figured maybe learning how to meditate would help. And it really did. . . . The process of meditation is a powerful one that allows you to look at yourself in the third person, not just during the meditation, but in the rest of your life." He described being in a moment and hearing a voice narrate what he was about to do, alerting him to signs that he wasn't being his true self. "That ability to be a step ahead of yourself, rather than a step behind yourself, for me was life changing." It all came from understanding himself better, his strengths and weaknesses, and who he really wanted to be, authentically.

I know everybody is telling you to meditate these days. It's starting to sound like a magic pill, sure to cure whatever ails you. And you might think meditation just isn't for you. But decades of research prove that mindfulness techniques work, so try to find one that can help you gain clarity about who you are and how you're showing up in different circumstances and roles.

If you want to signal to the world that you're open to new ideas and perspectives, show it by being transparently *you*. Work at being comfortable in your own skin. But one word of caution: don't use authenticity as an excuse. One of the big derailments in life is getting so entrenched in trying to defend who you are that it blinds you from opportunities to gain higher self-awareness and grow. Focus on the uniquely positive impact you can make as you continue to grow. It's a more fulfilling path than the alternative, and it's essential to being a lifelong learner.

Learning by Being Yourself—Your Best Self

- What are your strengths and talents? In just a few words, describe what being you looks like across all different kinds of situations.

- Where in your life right now—in specific parts of your job or in things you pursue outside of work—do those strengths and talents really shine? What's different about your learning attitude and mindset in those situations? What's different about your personal growth?

- Where in your life are you not being you, and why? What could you do about it?

Learn by seeking
new challenges

Chapter 19

"Not Yet"

As director of the Lift a Life Novak Family Foundation, Ashley Butler, my daughter, has proven herself to be an exceptional leader. She has a strong combination of analytical and creative-thinking skills that she has leveraged to develop and promote powerful, community-driven solutions to big challenges, like early childhood education, hunger, and diabetes care. One of the keys to her success is her ability to overcome a natural tendency many of us have to stay in our comfort zone. What Ashley has learned—and what you can do as an active learner—is to push herself, or let others gently push her, into uncharted territory.

When Indra Nooyi, former CEO of PepsiCo, agreed to be a guest on my podcast, I wanted her to talk about her new memoir, *Life in Full*. (If you want an advanced course in active learning, read her amazing book.) She writes about balancing career with family, learning to be a committed leader who's also a committed mother. I thought it would be a better episode if Ashley, rather than me, interviewed Indra. They have shared experiences, values, and passions, especially around women in leadership and improving the childcare infrastructure. I shared my idea with Indra, who agreed that Ashley's perspective would create a great conversation.

But when I asked Ashley if she would do it, I got a hard no. She was uncomfortable with the idea of interviewing Indra. She believed that Indra's experiences, ideas, and message deserved an informed, robust discussion, and her biggest fear was that she wouldn't do the conversation justice. She was afraid she would let both Indra and me down.

So I set out to help Ashley travel outside her comfort zone. First, I told her that her admiration for Indra made her the perfect person to have the conversation, *because* it was so important to her to do it justice. I reminded her that she had listened to every episode I had done and had interviewed me for an episode. She had a good sense of what makes an interesting interview. I told her that this was a once-in-a-lifetime opportunity to have whatever conversation she wanted with one of the most successful women in the world. If she didn't take it, she would regret it. But I also reminded her that Indra was also just a working mom who wanted to make a difference in the world—and that it was just a conversation between two people with shared passions.

But it was a final question I asked that tipped her thinking: "Have you ever considered for a minute that maybe you won't do a bad job?" I asked. "That maybe this could be a really fun, enjoyable experience?" The next morning, she agreed to do it, and of course she nailed it. Even more important, the feedback and recognition she got from Indra is helping her step outside her comfort zone more often.

Remember, part three here is all about *learning by doing*. **Active learners recognize that you learn very little by doing the same things over and over. You learn a lot by doing new things, and especially things that are outside your comfort zone.** Getting comfortable doing things that make you uncomfortable is how you achieve breakthroughs in your learning and your capacity. Active learners work on this every day.

It isn't always easy. Sometimes we feel like we're not ready for an uncomfortable challenge for tactical reasons. We don't have the skills yet. There's an easy fix for that: find a way to fill your gaps and learn what you need to take on the next important challenge in your career or life.

The harder-to-fix hurdle is that **none of us love trying new things, especially hard things**. Psychologists and economists call it the "status quo bias."[1] We're attracted to safety, certainty, and security, and we put higher value on things we *have* rather than things within reach, even if they're things we want. This makes new challenges—even exciting opportunities—stressful, which means they're likely to stir up negative emotions.

If that were the only thing holding you back, you could probably get motivated enough to break away from the status quo. But there's another, trickier mental anchor keeping you from trying: your limiting beliefs. In *Fast Forward*, Wendy Leshgold and Lisa McCarthy, two experienced leaders and coaches, explain that we *all* have limiting beliefs:

- About ourselves and what we're capable of

- About our circumstances and what they'll allow

- About other people and whether they'll help us succeed or not

Think about a time when you've said or thought something like, *I don't have what it takes to do that job,* or *My boss doesn't care about my career,* or *With my work schedule, I can't make time for . . .* The problem is that your brain interprets these beliefs as true, which cuts you off from the possibility that they aren't.

To overcome that hurdle, acknowledge the thinking that's holding you back, break down the beliefs and biases with facts and reality, and then replace them with more positive thoughts so that you can build the confidence and motivation to take action. Psychologists call this *cognitive reappraisal.*[2] Leshgold and McCarthy use three questions to help people get started:

1. "What is the limiting belief?" We don't usually spend a lot of time analyzing our own thinking, so it's important to start here.

2. "What is the cost of this belief in your life?" When we let our thinking limit what's possible for us, we always pay a price.

3. "[Imagine] you have let this belief go and it has no effect on your life anymore. . . What's now possible?" Imagining a world *without* limitations inspires us to take a leap of faith.[3]

This was the process I walked through with Ashley. She believed she wasn't up to the task of interviewing Indra. When she finally shared that with me, I prompted her to consider the costs, the missed opportunity, and the regret. **For active learners, this is the go-to question, because the cost of the status quo is usually stagnation in learning and growth, and that's more uncomfortable than the stress of change**. And then I asked Ashley to imagine a completely different, and much more positive, outcome from the one she envisioned.

As a sports performance coach, Jason Goldsmith, my coauthor for *Take Charge of You*, relies heavily on cognitive reappraisal, especially an approach called "reframing." It helps his clients shift their mindset and overcome the brain's negative, doubt-ridden, what-if thinking. His favorite reframing strategy is to turn your *nots* into *not-yets*. If you are considering a challenge and find yourself thinking about all the reasons that you're not ready or capable, add the word "yet" to the end of your arguments. Ashley might have said, "I haven't interviewed a CEO—yet." As Jason explained it, "One small word has changed the equation. 'Not done it before' no longer equals 'not possible.' And that change opens up room for belief to come in."

Jason's strategy and others like it help you manage the anxiety of not knowing how to do something or not knowing if you'll succeed. That was certainly true for Molly Fletcher, an agent who represented some of the most notable players and coaches across all sports. She's been called the "female Jerry Maguire," but early on she couldn't have known that that was her future. Choosing a male-dominated career created plenty of challenges, but she also created new challenges for herself right from the start. "So often in life we have to say, 'What's possible? What if?'" she told me. At her first job at a small agency that mostly took on *referrals*, she asked her boss if they had a growth plan. When he said no, she suggested they start *recruiting* clients instead. She drew up a business plan and two weeks later was off and running.

"I was down at Georgia Tech, leaning on a fence with scouts and coaches chewing tobacco and bubble gum, recruiting guys," she said. Being a competitive recruiter and growing her client list put her even more in the spotlight as a woman. "I was often the only woman [there]. I'd be behind the plate at batting practice and managers would yell at the guys who were coming over to talk to me. 'What are you doing hitting on that chick.' . . . My guys would say, 'It's my agent.' And the managers would say, 'Really?'"

The surprise and doubt could have fed a limiting belief that she wouldn't be able to succeed. And I'm sure she had unpleasant experiences along the way that she didn't share with me. But she actively fought that kind of thinking and continued to force herself to operate outside the comfort zone. "To me it was recognizing the opportunity to reframe the moment," she said. "From *Maybe I don't belong here. Maybe this isn't going to work. Maybe this is just a good old boys' space, and I can't add value*, to *I'm different. I think I can connect with these players in a way that is different. I think I can make their lives better in a way that's different.*" That active reframing kept her curious and open to possibility. And with each new challenge she tackled, from changing the direction of the company, to pushing into one new sport after another, to moving on from agenting to become a speaker, she has learned about herself, her industry, and her world.

Active learners embrace big challenges. For me, possibly the greatest challenge I ever *sought out* in my career was going for the chief operating officer role at Pepsi-Cola. I'd been tapped for other jobs, and they made logical sense—a marketing guy taking on new marketing positions. But I wanted one of the two COO posts that had opened up as part of a restructuring. Of course, as I mentioned in chapter 3,

I didn't have any operations experience. And I knew that as an applicant, I wouldn't have the resounding support of our chairman, Wayne Calloway.

PepsiCo executives were privileged to have quarterly lunches with Wayne. At one of these, he asked me where I saw myself going, career-wise. I was so happy he asked that I just blurted out, "I want to be president of a PepsiCo division."

"David, you're a really good *marketing* guy," he said. I knew what that meant: while he trusted my marketing abilities, he didn't see me as president material. He was a serious, quiet financial guy, and he saw me as a creative, emotion-driven, feel-good guy. I gently pushed back until he said, "I'll make you the president of marketing if you want." But it wasn't really the title of *president* that mattered to me. I wanted the big challenge of running a company, of being responsible for a P&L, of implementing ideas about culture, and all the personal and professional growth, the *learning,* that would come with it. I told Wayne all of this, but he kept pulling the conversation back to marketing.

If I was going to change his perception, I needed experience outside of marketing. The COO position, which opened not long after that lunch, was the perfect opportunity to keep my learning curve from flattening *and* to prove what I was capable of. I knew I wasn't the perfect fit for the job. I figured that what I lacked in experience I could make up for in dedication and a desire to learn. I begged Craig Weatherup, the president of the division, for the opportunity. Despite their hesitations, Wayne and Craig gave me a shot.

It helped that I made an offer that I hoped they couldn't refuse: "Give me the position for six months, and if you don't think I'm doing a great job, I'll go back and do anything you want me to do in marketing, no hard feelings, no questions asked. You can even fire me if you want to." I was taking charge of my career, and I think they both respected that.

The COO job was everything I hoped it would be. I learned about operations, of course, but I also learned more about how to learn, and learn fast. Step by step I tackled new challenges, expanded my leadership skills, and solved problems—and proved what I was capable of. I didn't get kicked out at the six-month mark, *and* I was successful enough that when they needed a president to turn around KFC, I got the nod. I obviously didn't know it at the time, but I was serving my apprenticeship for my eventual position as CEO of Yum!, another challenging role that I fought for.

So how did I convince myself to go outside my comfort zone?

Well, I'm not sure I could have told you this is what I was doing at the time, but one cognitive reappraisal technique I was using is called "examining the evidence," which is a way to combat our inclination to focus on the negative with facts. With reality, with proof. Objectively, I had ample proof that I could succeed and that I could get the support of Craig and Wayne. Craig had shown his faith in me before, and I knew Wayne respected my skills and talents. And while I didn't have operations experience, I knew our industry, our customers, and the problems we were facing. I also had years of leadership and experience stepping into dramatically different challenges and tackling hard-to-crack problems. The *evidence* offered more support for my success than my failure, even if my brain wanted me to doubt it. (I used this technique with Ashley on the podcast interview, too, trying to orient her to the reality that she had all the skills she needed to do a good job.)

Every time you step up to a new challenge and succeed, you're collecting evidence that you can use to convince yourself to tackle the *next* challenge. Pretty soon, it gets less uncomfortable and even becomes a habit.

For instance, when I left Yum! in 2016, officially I was retiring. But I had no intention of riding off into the sunset. I launched David Novak Leadership, worked to grow that business, and when I wanted to expand my reach even further, I found podcasts.

I knew even less about podcasts when I started than I did about being a COO when I started that job. I had never listened to one, never mind create one. But I dove in, did the research, asked a lot of questions, found the right support, and reached out to my network for potential guests. *How Leaders Lead* has become a top 1 percent business podcast, thanks to my ability to manage the anxiety of not knowing how to do something, and the support of others who helped me feel comfortable outside my comfort zone.

Now that the podcast is humming, I'm turning to new challenges. Right now, if you can believe it, that's writing country songs—but you'll have to wait until the end of the book to hear more about that.

Not everything new we do has to be a major departure from what we know. We're not compelled with every challenge to move miles away from our comfort zone. But when we tackle new challenges, we learn more about what we're capable of, and that opens up so many possibilities in our lives. More than that, when others see us stretching and learning, it inspires them to tackle *their* next opportunity, even when it seems like a long shot. And then, we're creating an environment where everybody grows and learns more together.

Learning by Seeking New Challenges

- What new challenge have you tackled in the past year? How did it turn out? What evidence can you collect from the experience that can help you the next time you have to get out of your own way and tackle a new challenge?

- Is there a new challenge that you're avoiding or hesitating on? What's the belief or thinking that's holding you back? How could you reframe the situation to make it easier to say yes?

- Is there a challenge you think you aren't ready for but that could be a big growth opportunity? What's the worst that could happen if it didn't work out? Could you find a way to limit the fallout?

Learn
by preparing

Chapter 20

Prime
Your Brain

If you've been reading this book straight through, you know I'm passionate about my podcast, *How Leaders Lead*. I've described the work we've put into building it, the experts we've consulted, and how we've benchmarked it against the best podcasts in our category. But I believe that the real, practical value of the podcast is generated by the work we put into each episode, especially how I personally prepare.

I begin before we even reach out to a potential guest. I know I need to make a compelling request, and that means learning a bit about them and why they would value talking with me about leadership. I know many potential guests, and I know they like to share their leadership wisdom. But some rarely give interviews, so I have to consider what it would take for them to trust me.

Once they say yes, the real work begins. I start by reading articles and watching videos of them speaking or being interviewed. If they've written a book, I'll read it or much of it. I'll ask common acquaintances for fresh stories and information. As I learn about them, I'm thinking about unique questions that will get to the heart of how they lead, and I'm gathering insights I can use to help them open up. I also think about the person and how they communicate and how I'll manage the conversation. (Right now, I'm learning more about artful interruption.)

I spend eight hours, give or take, getting ready for each episode. One of the podcasts that took me the longest to prepare for was my conversation with Jason Kelly, CEO of Ginkgo Bioworks. His company creates microorganisms that are used to create other products. That's some high-level biology—bordering on science fiction. Since I avoided science classes like the plague in college, I had to *really* dig in if I wanted to feel confident enough to even have the conversation. I had to read everything not once, but twice—and sometimes three times—before I understood it.

I also help my guests prepare. I don't share my questions because I want the conversation to flow naturally, but I do share my process, including the fact that they get approval of the final cut, so that they can relax and be their engaging selves. I also point them to some of my other guests who helped me produce great episodes, hoping they'll listen and learn.

What I'm doing, of course, is priming my brain, and the brains of my guests, so that we can have robust discussions that feed even more learning, for me and for everybody who listens. Yamini Rangan, CEO of HubSpot, picked up that baton and *ran* with it. She showed up for our discussion knowing as much about me as I did about her. She'd read my books, my bios, and articles I had written. I was motivated by her preparation to deliver my very best, and our combined preparation made for a dynamic and fun conversation. She reminded me how much it can mean to others when somebody shows up prepared, and how it can change their engagement and raise *their* curiosity level.

In *Fast Forward*, Wendy Leshgold and Lisa McCarthy write about the interplay between listening and curiosity. They explain how exposing ourselves to information, even when we think we aren't interested, can focus our attention and get the brain working to fill gaps in our knowledge:

> We tend to relate to our level of interest as black and white, as something out of our control. We find something interesting or we don't. If we don't, there's no point in exposing ourselves to it.

In fact, we can change our level of interest in almost anything. More than likely, if you think you aren't interested, you may not *know enough* to be interested. . . .

When we listen enough to learn a little information, our brain goes to work incorporating what we learned into what we already know. That process highlights gaps in our knowledge, which makes us wonder what we're missing.[1]

This lesson is true for all kinds of information gathering, not only listening (although that's one of the best). As I prepare for a podcast, the more I learn about a guest, the more curious I become, and that makes for a better discussion. Preparation boosts our curiosity and primes the brain for new ideas and information.

Active learners know that good preparation helps us get the most learning out of any experience. We learn throughout the process of preparing, and we learn more when we're prepared. When I'm prepared for my podcasts, I can be present and engaged. I can listen fully, and I can guide the conversation better. That helps me uncover more ideas so that we all learn more.

Jim Nantz, the Emmy Award–winning sports commentator, operates with the same mindset. "Every show is your most important show," he told me. "You never take anything for granted. . . . Out of respect for your audience and out of respect for the subject you're covering, you have to do the full, detailed research." He still creates his own spotting boards, or summaries of the important details of each player in a game he's calling. He writes them out by hand because it helps him remember the information better. And while others in the industry keep the details at a high level, Jim gets into the minutiae of their lives and their stats, color-coded on each board. "That depth of knowledge is the only way I know how to go about it. . . . When it comes to my job, it's my responsibility, so no one's going to do my research for me."

In *Shift Your Mind*, Brian Levenson, performance coach for athletes and executives, explores the differences between preparation and performance. The mindset we need for each is different, he says. "Preparation involves learning, growing, and improving, whereas performance is pure execution, carrying out an action or pattern of behavior designed to achieve a goal."[2] Jim Nantz is able to perform— pulling stories and stats seemingly out of nowhere while responding to the most recent play and cuing up the expert analyst at his side— because of the time he invests in learning, improving, and analyzing (he even listens to and critiques his own broadcasts).

Peyton Manning, one of the greatest quarterbacks of all time, told me that he once had a coach who told him that he was so slow, he couldn't run out of sight in a week. Peyton knew he wasn't the strongest or fastest player on the field, so he needed an advantage. "Preparation was where I got my edge in football. I couldn't out-throw anybody. I certainly couldn't outrun anybody. . . . But I could at least out-prepare them."

When we prepare, we are building neural pathways that make taking action easier and smoother. Instead of being focused on performing those actions in the moment, we are free to focus on what's happening in front of us, glean important information, and respond accordingly. Then, when an opportunity arises to take our learning to the next level, to pursue a new challenge, to do something new and different, we're ready.

Brian Roberts, the CEO of Comcast, calls this "hanging around the rim." In my work with him on the Comcast board, I've marveled at his ability to spot the next opportunity and jump on it. He has told me that he goes to as many conferences as he can, especially the tech conferences. He spends time in Hollywood. He networks with content creators and entertainers. He's always looking for the next deal, the next smart partnership, the new way of thinking about content delivery. He positions himself to learn, meet people, and be informed so that he'll be ready to act when the time comes. It's a lot of time spent preparing for a moment that *might* show up, but it's an investment that has made him highly successful.

Of course, **not all preparation is equal. Good preparation is purposeful,** as the purposeful practice psychologist Anders Ericsson discovered in his research into peak performers. He focuses on deliberate practice in his book *Peak*, but that's simply purposeful practice with the help of a coach in a well-established field. "Because deliberate practice was developed specifically to help people become among the best in the world at what they do," he wrote, "it is the most powerful approach to learning that has yet been discovered."[3] Take Brian Roberts. His efforts might sound haphazard, as if he was just "hanging around" smart, creative people waiting for lightning to strike, but he was highly focused on the goal of discovering the next big idea that would help Comcast beat a competitor to market, attract a new audience, or innovate in some way. That deliberate focus has helped him learn vital ideas and information.

Anders studied how people become top-of-the-field experts, but I think three of his four attributes of purposeful practice apply to any kind of serious preparation:

- Work toward a specific goal.

- Be intensely focused on improvement (or learning).

- Get out of your comfort zone.

This could easily be a definition of active learning. When I'm preparing for a podcast, I'm ticking most of those boxes, on some level.

Jack Nicklaus, who many think is the greatest golfer of all time, certainly did. He was highly specific, deliberate, and focused on challenging himself. "I think being prepared is probably the most important thing in any walk of life," he told me. For instance, early every year, he focused specifically on preparing for the Masters, playing courses that would help him improve his play at the Augusta National Golf Club course where the Masters is held annually. He shared proof of the power of preparation by telling a story of a time when he *wasn't* prepared. At the 1985 US Open, he missed the cut for the first time in nearly twenty years, failing to qualify to play in the final rounds of the tournament. He admitted that he hadn't prepared. He had been busy working as a commentator for ABC. "The only thing worse than missing the cut," he said, "is to have to stay around . . . and talk about everybody else playing in the tournament while you're watching." As a consolation, he and his wife, Barbara, went to McDonald's for a hamburger. Barbara noticed a fitting message on the Happy Meal cups at the restaurant. The next day, when Jack woke up, one of those cups was sitting next to his bed holding his morning coffee. The words of wisdom? "There's no excuse for not being properly prepared." Because as Jack said, "If you're not prepared, you're not gonna perform."

For years, I had an embroidered pillow in my bedroom that just said, "PLAN." It was a reminder to take time every night to prepare for the following day—to review my meetings, read analyst reports, check in on major projects, and more. I wanted to walk into every day ready to listen, learn, and contribute. Every morning, I prepared to deliver on that goal. I exercised, journaled, and focused on gratitude. I did all of that with the goal of delivering my best to the million or so people around the world who relied on me to make good decisions for the company.

And I still follow this preparation ritual every single day, with the same high expectations—because you never knew exactly what the day will bring or what opportunities to learn more might show up.

Learning by Preparing

- Have you ever found yourself becoming more and more curious or interested in something when you've been forced to learn a bit about it? How could you leverage that effect in your life or work?

- Think of a time when you were unprepared. (If it can happen to Jack Nicklaus, it can happen to any of us.) How did you feel in the moment? Where was your attention or focus? Do you think you might have missed out on an opportunity to learn?

- When you are well prepared for a situation, performance, conversation, or meeting, how is your focus different? How is your mindset, or your openness to ideas, different?

Learn by doing the hard things

Chapter 21

The Foundation That Can't Be Swept Away

Here's a favorite quote of mine that I have framed in my office:

> The easy way is efficacious and speedy, the hard way arduous
> and long. But, as the clock ticks, the easy way becomes harder,
> and the hard way becomes easier. And as the calendar records
> the years, it becomes increasingly evident that the easy way
> rests hazardously upon shifting sands, whereas **the hard way
> builds solidly a foundation of confidence that cannot be
> swept away.**

Who said this? Colonel Sanders.

When I became president of KFC, his legacy loomed large. He made the business a success on a shoestring budget while maintaining the highest standards. After a newly built interstate bypass ruined his own successful restaurant, he sold his *original* recipe for fried chicken door to door, at the age of sixty-five. Over ten years, he built up Kentucky Fried Chicken to more than six hundred stores in the United States, Canada, and England.

Colonel Sanders was an active learner, and active learners understand that taking the easy way out, avoiding the hardest work, or looking for shortcuts truncates your learning and limits your results. **You cut out the "doing" that would have given you the learning.**

Getting to the most important insights and the best results often means taking the hard way. Doing the hard things also helps you fight against the tyranny of incrementalism. There's a classic fable about napkins in the food service industry. To save money, a restaurant owner decided to buy cheaper napkins that were a quarter of an inch smaller. It saved him a bit of money. The next year, seeing the success of the cost-cutting, he bought thinner napkins and saved a bit more. The following year, he went even smaller—and his napkins expense doubled. Customers were taking two or three when they used to take one. When companies focus too much on cost-cutting, which can lead to corner-cutting, as a path to profit, they eventually lose their advantage. Lasting, sustainable growth comes from *doing the hard work* of improving your products and making your customers happy.

The same thing can happen to us as individuals. Taking the easy way sets you on a course that may lead you somewhere very different from where you hoped to end up. And it can become a habit faster than you realize.

Author Ryan Holiday wrote in his bestseller *Ego Is the Enemy*, "Greatness comes from humble beginnings; it comes from grunt work."[1] It's equally true for businesses and people. I learned the lesson early. My parents only had high school educations, but they did the hard work to improve our lives. My mom got a job as a bookkeeper, taught herself accounting, and eventually became a company controller.

My dad spent our years on the road advancing in the National Geodetic Survey, eventually working in the DC office. He was the only one of his colleagues who didn't have an engineering degree. Imagine him decades before, at just fifteen years old, leaving home for the summer and traveling to Nebraska to work for the railroad. He lied and said he was sixteen to get a job painting bridges. This is how he described it in his memoir, *Home Is Everywhere*:

> At first, they just had me painting the side of the bridge from a scaffold. Then my job changed, and I would get on this little sled that attached to the bridge's diagonal beams, lying down on my stomach, and paint the beam as I went down. It was like sliding down a banister, only I used a rope to control my speed so I wouldn't slide down too fast. I wasn't strapped in or nothing. I just had to hold on. . . . On my sled, I'd have this bucket full of paint. Well, back then they mixed the paint with creosote to make it last longer. When it got hot, the creosote would just heat up and burn my skin—mostly my face, since I was lying on my stomach with my face right in it as I painted. All summer long I painted bridges, and my face was burnt to a crisp by the end.[2]

His willingness to do hard things enabled him to support his family later in life. He taught us that work ethic, and it became the foundation to my success. I mowed yards as a kid and my dad would inspect my work, sending me back if I hadn't gotten the details right so that I *earned* my $3. From the time I was in high school and all through college, I took whatever job I could get to make money. One summer, I worked for the North Kansas City School District cleaning the schools. I had to clean every desk. The bottoms were especially unpleasant. In college, I got a job picking up trash and sweeping floors at a local strip mall. I earned a paycheck, but I also learned to appreciate hard work and the people who do it. (And I learned the power of recognition. Even in those jobs, which I saw as temporary, it meant something when somebody gave me an "attaboy." I learned that every job has dignity when we treat the person doing the job with dignity.)

The lessons carried forward throughout my career. As a leader, if I visited a restaurant and saw a piece of trash on the ground, I picked it up. If I saw some un-bused tables, I bused them. Every time I took a new leadership position, at Pizza Hut, Pepsi-Cola, or KFC, I spent time doing the core jobs. I made pizzas, rode delivery trucks, and breaded and fried chicken. I regularly served customers. It gave me greater appreciation for the work required, the people doing it, and how my decisions would affect them. I was also building connections with the team members, which encouraged them to share what they were learning with me. By doing the hard things, I created a culture and atmosphere that helped me learn more.

Leaders are taught to delegate, but you have to avoid becoming disconnected, especially from the fundamental work of the business and the people making it happen. Tony Xu, founder and CEO of DoorDash, carried that sensibility into building his business. He told me that he also learned his work ethic from his parents, who moved from China to the United States when Tony was five years old. The family had no savings and very little income as his father completed a degree in mathematics. His mother, who had been a doctor in China, worked three jobs for twelve years to support them, saving every penny she could while earning *her* degree. Eventually, she used the savings to open a medical clinic that she still runs today.

So, maybe it's not surprising that Tony and his cofounders bootstrapped DoorDash, financially and operationally. "One of the things I've always believed in business or other walks of life is you have to be able to understand things at the lowest level of detail. And there's no way to do that if you don't do every job in that world." For the first eighteen months of the business, he and his cofounders did every single delivery. "While classmates of mine [at Stanford, where he had just earned his MBA] were moving on and taking great vacations, I was schlepping hummus from my Honda."

And he was *learning* about logistics and delivery—things that made a real difference in DoorDash's ability to become one of the early and biggest services of its kind. To this day, every person in the company spends time every month doing deliveries and customer support.

If you become disconnected from the hard work that needs to be done, you might stop learning about the things that matter most.

I recognize that I was fortunate, in the same way that Tony Xu was fortunate. Not everybody gets the education in hard work that we got early in life. Most of us put off doing hard things because of the power of our "expediency bias" and the Hedonic principle. David Rock, psychologist, author, and founder of the NeuroLeadership Institute, explains:

> We are wired to move toward things that make us feel good and away from things that make us feel uncomfortable. Our brains tag effort as bad because it's hard work. They default to what feels "normal"—the networks that tell us where and how to travel through our daily existence. Those networks are so deep in our thinking that when we're traveling a new and challenging path—regardless of what that path is—our wheels default back to the worn-in grooves. And yet, we know hard actions can have tremendous benefits.[3]

So how do we circumvent our thinking and make it just a bit easier to do the hard things? One important strategy that Rock mentions is to **try to do hard things when we're in a good mood, when the brain is less likely to throw up resistance.** And that's why the first chapter of this section is to learn by pursuing *joy*.

This might seem reflexively obvious, but another strategy for doing hard things is to just do them. Motivation often grows out of action. Sometimes, you just have to force it.

Arnold Palmer once stayed at our house when he came to town to attend the Kentucky Derby. He and Wendy were having coffee one morning when he broke a glass. He asked her where the broom and dustpan were, and she said, "I can't have Arnold Palmer cleaning up a mess in my kitchen."

"Honey," he replied, "I've been cleaning up messes I've made in kitchens ever since I was a kid in Latrobe, Pennsylvania." That mindset of being responsible for doing even the small things he might not want to do made a big difference in his career. For instance, he made a point of making sure that every time he signed an autograph, it was legible. He thought, *What's the point in signing autographs if people can't read the name? What message does that send to the person who has come to support me?* It might not seem like a hard thing, but when you're exhausted, frustrated, or anxious at the end of a tournament day, signing autographs might be the very last thing you want to do. He would do it anyway.

Another strategy comes from your brain's love of autonomy. You can try giving yourself a choice. **Choosing to do something is a lot more motivating than *having* to do something. It's important to focus on the benefit of the hard choice and the cost of the easy choice.** David Rock gave this example: "Do I want to experiment with a new project management tool that might make things easier for my team next week, or do I want to stick with the same spreadsheet that a former employee established that none of us feel great about anyway?"

Sometimes we don't have a choice in the hard things we have to do. But we have a choice in where they take us. We can *choose* to turn our adversity or obstacles into an advantage for ourselves or other people. Jon Rahm, who has been ranked the number one golfer in the world, has a swing that's widely regarded as perfect, and it's that way because he's consistently done the hard things. He was born with a club foot on his right leg, which is part of what turned him on to golf since he never could run or jump as well as other kids. He learned to turn that into a positive. He grew up in a small town in northern Spain, hardly a golf mecca, but worked hard to get recruited by Arizona State. He had never been to America until the day he showed up as a freshman, and he spoke almost no English. Still, he earned his degree before going pro and becoming the first European to win the US Open and the Masters tournament.

My wife, Wendy, has been through some brutally hard medical experiences because of her type 1 diabetes. Learning from doing the hard things along the way is allowing her to build the Wendy Novak

Diabetes Institute into a place that makes the disease easier for others. She makes this choice every day. Recently, a kid at the center said he wanted to talk to her—I guess because her name was on the building where he was spending a lot of his time. Wendy reassured him and gave him hope that he'll be able to do what she has—defy expectations at every turn. That's only been possible because she has consistently done the hard things and maintained a positive attitude as she did.

And if you need more fodder for convincing yourself away from the easy or expedient choice, **consider all the cautionary tales, including from your own life, about what happens when we delay or avoid doing the hard things.** Wells Fargo's story is an enlightening one. At the lower levels of management, leaders had pushed unrealistic sales quotas that led to fraud, billions in fines, and a damaged reputation. The company didn't have the right controls in place to catch it before the problem spun out of control. When Charlie Scharf took over as CEO in 2019, four years after the initial scandal broke, Wells Fargo was still struggling to come out from under a cloud of consent orders, or special dictates from the Consumer Financial Protection Bureau (CFPB), about the problems a company has to fix and the actions it has to take. Because few of the consent orders had been completely resolved, regulators roamed Wells Fargo offices constantly, assessing progress and analyzing work. One of the consent orders restricted the company from growing the business—assets under management—until big regulatory infrastructure and internal control issues were worked out. It was a huge blow.

Charlie knew coming into the role that the consent orders had to be dealt with as fast as possible. This isn't fun work. It's not exciting or innovative. It's hard—really hard. The only way through was to hunker down and do all of the hard things *well* so that the company could regain its credibility. And that's what he and the critical teams involved in the transformation have done. They made so much progress, and much faster progress, after Charlie came on board that the CFPB has been steadily lifting orders. There's still a lot of work to do, but everybody, including industry analysts, has much more confidence about the future now that they're doing the hard things.

When I asked Charlie what he's learned from this, he told me that the process has been a tremendous reminder of the obvious—you have to get the basics right, have the right people in place, and have the correct structure in place. But the big lesson is that when there's a tough problem to solve, you must generate a sense of urgency.

Because the longer you delay doing the hard things, the harder they become. And the harder they become, the more bogged down you are in minutiae and rework, making it harder to focus on the essential lessons you should be discovering.

I've learned versions of that lesson more than once in my life. For instance, I put off surgery I needed for my Achilles tendon for about five years. I did everything I could to avoid it—all kinds of painful therapy, platelet shots, exercises, stretches, and on and on. All I could think about was the small percentage of surgeries that didn't go well, causing chronic pain or a permanent limp. The thought that I might not be able to play golf again was scary. Eventually, though, the pain became too much.

Eight weeks after finally having the surgery, I was almost pain-free. But I had put up with five years of pain trying to avoid it. Putting off the hard thing just put off the solution, which was there the whole time. In avoiding the hard thing, all I really accomplished was avoiding learning.

Learning by Doing the Hard Things

- What is one of the hardest things you've chosen to do? How did you motivate yourself to do it? What were some of the important lessons you learned?

- Where in your life does "expediency bias"—the tendency to focus on the easiest next step rather than the best next step—have the biggest impact? Where does the comfortable, normal option usually win out? What strategy do you think would help you choose the hard thing instead?

- Is there a hard thing you're currently avoiding or delaying? What's keeping you from it? What could be possible if you just did it?

Learn by doing
the right thing

Chapter 22

The WSJ Test

I've had one brush with criminal activity, when I was ten.

I loved to play army, and one of my favorite Christmas presents one year was a canteen. I used it all the time—until I lost the lid, which felt tragic to a ten-year-old boy.

Magically, I found a replacement a couple of weeks later at the store where my mom had bought the canteen. When she noticed the lid at home later, she asked me where I'd found it, but I couldn't lie. I took it, I told her. You can guess what happened next: she marched me back to the store to return the lid and apologize to the manager.

I learned that day that shoplifting wouldn't be my vocation, and more important, that it's never too late to do the right thing. You can always go back, say you're sorry, and try to make things right.

Running a company that had over a million team members spread over 112 countries reinforced that idea for me, but it's something that I first learned as a kid, as we moved from town to town. Good values are universal and eternal. ("Don't steal" is a pretty basic one.)

Of course, *whether* or *how* we live those values can vary dramatically. When I was leading Yum! and teaching a leadership program to employees, I used to share this value statement from another company, because it's so noble and universal:

RESPECT: We treat others as we would like to be treated ourselves. We do not tolerate abusive or disrespectful treatment. INTEGRITY: We work with customers and prospects openly, honestly, and sincerely. COMMUNICATION: We have an obligation to communicate. Here, we take the time to talk with one another . . . and to listen. EXCELLENCE: We are satisfied with nothing less than the very best in everything we do. We will continue to raise the bar for everyone. The great fun here will be for all of us to discover just how good we can really be.

Can you guess the company? It comes from Enron—a company so corrupt it imploded and destroyed the financial lives and retirements of thousands of its employees, defying every value named here as it did. Way back on August 28, 1869, the *Harrisburg Telegraph* of Harrisburg, Pennsylvania, printed this nugget of wisdom: "There is a difference between doing a thing *right*, and doing the right *thing*. One individual may be engaged in a very bad work, and yet do his work well."—Enron—"Another may be engaged in a laudable undertaking and do his work very poorly. The true maxim is, 'do the right thing right.'"

I like to say, "Do the right things *and the right things happen.*" You'll build a reputation as somebody who can be trusted, and you'll free yourself from the burden of constantly looking backward with regret instead of forward with hope. Together, these two outcomes expand learning in our life. People share more with us, and our outlook is more positive and future focused.

Doing the right thing is the gift you give yourself. How do we know if we're making the right choices, doing the right things? Being an active learner requires us to tell the truth *to* ourselves *about* ourselves, to honestly assess what we see in the mirror.

Sometimes we need a bit more accountability than we can muster alone or even as a group. At Yum! our CFO Dave Deno would ask an important question whenever we were navigating a tough decision: Does this pass the *Wall Street Journal* test? That is, **if this shows up on the front page of the *Wall Street Journal* tomorrow, will we be happy?**

Will we be proud of what it says about us as a company? We asked that question about how we went about cutting costs, how we moved people out of the company, and just about anything where the right thing wasn't as obvious as "don't steal."

You can develop a version of the test for your tough decisions. Maybe it's, **"Would I feel good or proud when explaining this decision to my spouse, my child, or my boss?"** Or maybe it's, "If I had to stand up and share this at a team meeting, at a conference, or in church, would I be comfortable and proud?"

None of the odd jobs I had growing up—mowing lawns, construction, janitorial work—paid particularly well, so when I saw an ad saying you could make at least $75 a day as a salesperson, I just about ran to downtown Kansas City and applied. The job turned out to be selling encyclopedias door-to-door. Someone dropped me off in the middle of a nearby town and then picked me up at the end of the day; it was up to me to knock on doors and make something happen. My first day, I sold two sets of encyclopedias, a pretty good start.

The next day I sold another set, and in two days, I had made $225! That was more than I would make in a week in my first job after college some years later.

On the third day, I quit. I didn't have a good feeling in my gut about what I was doing. I felt like I was selling encyclopedias to people who didn't need them. I sold one set to an older woman without kids who was just happy to have someone to talk to for a while. I think she bought the books to thank me.

I learned I was good at selling, but I didn't really believe in how I was doing it. The money was compelling, but I knew I needed to pay attention to the little voice telling me that the people buying might come to regret their decision. I wasn't necessarily doing the WSJ test explicitly, but I knew if I went home and described to my parents what I was doing and who I was selling to, I wouldn't be proud.

Years later, I should have listened to my gut when I blew off a dinner with Leo Kiely, the head of marketing for Frito-Lay. Leo had recommended me for the senior vice president of marketing position at

Pizza Hut after working at an ad agency. He opened a door into Pep-siCo and gave me the most important opportunity of my career. I was going to be in New York, and he and I planned to meet up for dinner. But then I got a call from Roger Enrico, the CEO of PepsiCo, asking me to have dinner with *him*. My ambition kicked in, and I canceled on Leo. I apologized, but our relationship was never the same after. Decades later, I still carry the regret.

Our toughest decisions are often those kinds of in-the-moment choices. We have to lean on our values and ideals then, which means we need to know what they are. We think our general sense of right and wrong will be enough, but in complicated, high-pressure situations, that may not be enough. For Mark Esper, former secretary of defense under President Donald Trump, who faced one complex situation after another, his clarity on this point was crucial. He told me that he is more loyal to the two oaths he has taken—his oath to defend the US Constitution and his oath to love, honor, and care for his wife—than to anything else. So, when the president suggested sending active-duty military troops to control protesters in cities in 2020, his decision was a clear and immediate no, because it violated the Constitution. This wasn't the first or last time his commitment to uphold the Constitution clarified his decisions, but it was one of the most public.

Every time you push yourself to do the right thing, you're rediscovering your values. You're learning to translate them into action. When Yum! started up, the Taco Bell franchisees didn't like some of the parameters of the new company and threatened to try a hostile takeover of the division and create a separate company. I worked hard to make inroads with them, but I hadn't yet earned their trust when we encountered our first big crisis.

An environmental organization released a report saying that StarLink, a genetically modified organism, had been found in Kraft Taco Bell taco shells, which were manufactured by Kraft and sold in grocery stores. The franchisees never liked the fact that the Kraft-manufactured Taco Bell products even existed in grocery stores, because it potentially ate into their revenue. But PepsiCo corporate had signed the licensing agreement, and Yum! inherited it. The Food and Drug Administration had not explicitly approved StarLink for human consumption, so this became a national news story.

It didn't matter that StarLink wasn't likely to hurt anyone or that it was never found in our *restaurant* taco shells. What mattered was that our customers were scared to eat Taco Bell because Kraft immediately recalled its product. The franchisees weren't benefiting from the licensing agreement because it was a corporate deal, but they paid the price. Sales, which were already flat, dropped another 20 to 25 percent.

Some franchisees were near bankruptcy—the publicity was killing them. A mutiny was brewing. Contractually, we weren't obligated to help. But if we didn't, there would be obvious consequences for Yum!

Some at Yum! felt that the company should not assume the risk of bailing out the franchisees. If stores went under, we could always buy them back at a low price. Others, including me, thought that didn't feel right.

Here's a useful test: as much as I appreciate the work of attorneys, the law is just the first rung of basic good behavior. Truly ethical decisions and actions usually take us much further up the ladder. **If you're turning to a contract or legal standard to tell if you're doing the right thing, chances are you're not climbing high enough to see if you are.**

I worked with the team at Yum! to keep climbing until we came up with a plan that *did* feel right. We set up a team to work with the banks to restructure franchisees' debts. We sued the supplier that provided the taco shells and then gave the money we recovered, which was a lot, back to the franchisees. And we absorbed all the legal and administrative costs of this process. All we asked in return was that they agree not to sue us or go public against us. If we were going to do right by them and be their partner in this crisis, they needed to do right by us.

The good news is that the hard-working franchisees hung on, and sales eventually turned around. In fact, Taco Bell became the second-most-profitable quick-service brand in the United States, behind only McDonald's.

Following the crisis, the Taco Bell franchisees asked me to attend a special meeting where something incredible happened. These people, who just a few years earlier had threatened mutiny, brought me in to thank us for our support. They called what we had done for them "heroic" and gave me a four-foot-high Superman statue with my face on it. Every one of them thanked me personally, telling me things like, "My family wouldn't have its business today if it weren't for you." It was one of the most emotional experiences of my career.

By doing that right thing, we learned. We learned lessons about how to effectively face a crisis—and Yum! certainly faced more crises in the future. We learned about the strengths and weaknesses of the Taco Bell restaurants and franchise groups, which allowed us to support their success better going forward.

I'm happy to know that that same ethos exists at Yum! today. At the start of the pandemic, when businesses were forced to shut down and restaurants were hit especially hard, David Gibbs, the current CEO, and his team told the franchisees to stop paying their royalties. Yum! would give them all a grace period until the tide had turned. Every franchisee paid back 100 percent of the royalties they owed. Trying to drag royalties out of them wouldn't have worked anyway, so why not show the franchisees loyalty and support? Because David did, the franchisees returned it.

To use a business cliché, David walked the talk. But when Eric Harvey published *Walk the Talk* almost thirty years ago, the title wasn't quite the cliché that it is now. But the concept still resonates. The core idea of Harvey's book is that **you may judge yourself by your intentions, but others judge you by your actions. That's how you build your reputation, and your reputation influences what's possible in your work and life.**

We all know that not everybody operates by that principle.

In 2015, I had the great honor to receive the Horatio Alger Award, which was created to recognize people who have achieved great things by overcoming adversity and living its ideals of perseverance, integrity, and excellence. One of the neat things was that I received the award the same year as the youngest person to ever receive it. That person was Elizabeth Holmes of Theranos.

I sat on a panel with her and other honorees and answered questions from recipients of the scholarships that the association gives. I was so impressed with her answers and story that afterward I suggested she consider joining the board of one of the companies I work with. And like so many other people, I was equally disappointed when I learned how she had deceived investors, broken laws, and ruined the lives of some of her employees, taking them down with her. She acted without regard for anybody but herself and will end up serving eleven years in prison.

There's a lot of tragedy in this story, but here's a loss that isn't much talked about: the lost learning and potential. She had built a team of smart and talented people. She had attracted incredible resources. Those two things *plus* good choices could have created an explosion of powerful, innovative ideas that would resonate for decades to come. Who knows what might have been possible. Who knows how many lives could have been changed. Who knows what "right things" were lost.

We're most likely to step over the line, or take a running leap over it, when we're backed into a corner. Desperate situations are challenges to our values. You can help your future self to do the right thing by avoiding them as much as possible through good planning and preparation. Consider things that can go wrong and decide in advance (instead of in the moment) how you'll handle them while staying true to your values. You can also avoid them by tackling problems as soon as you find them so that they don't grow into catastrophes (something I'll dig into in the next chapter). I liked to tell people, "You'll never get fired for bringing me a problem, but you'll definitely get fired for covering one up." We can't prepare for every complicated situation that might require a tough decision, but we can try to arm ourselves with the right resources, information, and values-based foundation.

This is vital, because over time, depending on environments and circumstances and your own choices, your sense of right and wrong can suffer from stepwise degradation. You stray over the line, stray a bit further the next time, justifying one bad action after another. Stray too far over the line and you can lose sight of it entirely. Eventually, you lose the ability to know what doing the right thing looks like.

The best thing that happens when we do the right thing is that we feel good about our choices and the impact we're having on the world, and that inspires us to keep doing the right thing. Values aren't something you write down on a piece of paper and then put in a drawer or hang on the wall. Values are something you *use* to take good action. It isn't always the easy choice, but it's always the best choice and the one that helps you learn the most powerful lessons.

Learning by Doing the Right Thing

- Was there a time in your life when you didn't do the right thing and knew it? What was the result for you? For others?

- When you've had the courage to do the right thing in the past, what did you learn about yourself, others, or a situation?

- Are you struggling with a decision or challenge right now? If you strip away every complicating factor, what would doing the right thing look like? Is there a version of the *Wall Street Journal* test that you could apply?

Chapter 23

From Pain to Possibility

Most of my career moves reflect a theme: I took jobs with organizations that were experiencing trouble. Those might seem like jobs to avoid, but I have never felt that way. When you become responsible for a team or a company at the top of its game, your job is *Don't screw it up.* That always sounded harder or scarier than *Find a way to fix the problems.* I like fixing problems; in fact, fixing one big problem after another at PepsiCo led to my dream job with Yum!

Solving problems and active learning go hand in hand. **You learn *by* tackling problems—in two ways. One, you spot them on the horizon and then learn so that you can prevent them from affecting you. Or two, if they're already on top of you, you learn so that you can solve them as effectively and efficiently as possible.**

While most people prefer to *avoid* problems—ignoring the signs that they're coming or explaining them away—active learners have a different mindset. They consistently tackle the problems they see.

That's why the learning opportunities that come from taking on problems are woven into the curriculum of our Lead4Change program. It includes modules that help students learn to "anticipate the hurdles" and "overcome barriers to success." While students are tackling big problems by raising awareness of homelessness, addressing environmental challenges, supporting recently resettled immigrants in their town, improving the quality of food available at local food banks, and more, they're also learning so much more. They're learning how to bring people on board, organize, and break down challenges. They're learning more about the people they're trying to help and what other problems they face. They're learning how to solve problems better the next time. And maybe they're falling in love with the mission they're tackling.

People and companies that look for problems to solve see two big benefits, according to Uri Levine, founder of Waze and author of *Fall in Love with the Problem, Not the Solution.* "If you follow this path and your solution works, it's guaranteed that you're creating value. But when you tell people that you are going to address this problem, and you ask them what they think about it, you kind of sign up for a mission." And sometimes, you discover new and bigger problems to tackle next.

Daniel Lubetzky, the founder of KIND Snacks, founded his first food company, PeaceWorks, during a fellowship in Israel. He was working to foster economic cooperation between Israel and its Arab neighbors. When he learned that an Israeli company making sauces and spreads was going out of business because its costs were too high, he convinced it to buy its materials from Arab manufacturers and Palestinian farmers. PeaceWorks was born.

Maintaining the company, especially in the early years, was difficult. "What kept me going was my sense of mission: I was in this to help build a footing for peace," he wrote in his book, *Do the KIND Thing.*[1] Today, solving the challenge of kindness—the lack of it or the lack of understanding of what it means to be kind—is a big part of his mission, and it's woven into the work the company does and its social responsibility efforts.

"It was part of our mission from the very beginning to try to increase empathy and kindness and to make kindness a state of mind," he told me. "A lot of what we invest in, from our philanthropy and from our marketing, is trying to help people be more kind toward one another and make kindness front of mind, to become the trait that we want all of our children to aspire to. . . . We can't achieve that just by selling product. We do have to create a community and a movement of people that are part of the journey with us."

Lubetzky's learning through his problem-driven mission has turned into big success for the company, which itself engages in active learning to solve the problem of creating healthy, delicious, whole-food snacks.

The first step in becoming a problem-tackler is getting to the right mindset, especially for big problems that require a team effort. It's not unusual for big problems to seem unsolvable and cause teams to feel so defeated by their scope that they shoot down every solution. When I became COO of Pepsi-Cola in 1992, operations was one of those problems. Nearly every aspect of operations needed improvement, from forecasting to pricing to loading and delivery. It was so bad that we could have performed better if we had just put our operations money in a savings account and collected interest.

Before I came on board, the CEO had decided to gather the whole company, more than six thousand people, at the Dallas Convention Center to discuss the problems. I was slated to be the after-dinner speaker.

The meeting was largely about pain—customer pain, employee pain, financial pain. All anyone seemed to be talking about was all the things going wrong. That wasn't my style. When I stood up in front of the group, I said nothing. For ten seconds, absolute silence. Finally, I broke it: "There's one thing I want you to know. This is one great company, and I don't want anyone here to forget it."

The place exploded.

Ever since the Ray Charles "You got the right one, baby, uh-huh" Pepsi commercial that I had worked on, I had become known around the company as "the Uh-Huh Guy." I had leveraged the "uh-huh" refrain as part of a massive marketing campaign, and it became a pop-culture catchphrase. As I stood in front of those six thousand people, something amazing emerged. As I continued to talk—not about problems, but about solutions—people started to respond with "uh-huh." It started with a few people, but soon, all six thousand people were joining in. I'd say, "And then we're going to do this," and they'd all say, "Uh-huh!" "And then we're going to do that," and they'd all say, "Uh-huh!" The convention center had turned into an old-fashioned tent revival meeting.

We came out of our slump shortly after that, and I'd like to think that speech put a little fire in our bellies. It didn't solve the problems, but it did shift the mindset from *insurmountable pile of problems* to *a challenge we can take on.* From *pain* to *possibility.* And as we knocked down one problem after another, we learned more and more, making the next problem a little easier to tackle.

I learned a great technique for shifting people's thinking from "not possible" to "what might be possible" called *flip the script,* from Scott Bergren, former CEO of Pizza Hut. When someone would say, "That can't be done" or "That's impossible," he would say, "Well, what would *you* do to solve the problem?"

While getting to the right mindset is important, active learners know that it's a secondary challenge. **The first challenge is that you can't tackle problems that you don't know exist,** so they go looking for them, often by going to customers or other stakeholders. They might uncover problems that are already in play or that are looming on the horizon.

In my experience as an active learner, I've noticed that people aren't always good at coming to you with ideas for improvement. But they are good at telling you what's frustrating them. That's how you uncover problems that need solving. At Yum! we initiated conversations with our customers through problem-detection studies, and it helped us learn what they needed from us most so that we could make important product innovations.

Note that we didn't call our process "solution mining studies" or something like it. We needed to find the problems first. Jeff Lawson, cofounder and CEO of Twilio, a company that supports apps with back-end cloud communication services (think of text messaging within the Airbnb app, for example), told me he thinks of businesses like prospectors, out in the world digging for that gold—the thing that will differentiate them and help them grow. But, and this is crucial, "The gold isn't the solution," he said. "The gold is the problem. Finding a really big, hairy, important, hard problem that your customers need solved—*that's* the biggest challenge of business, not how you solve it." Individuals can operate this way, too—and active learners get that. They see the opportunity, the *value,* in problems, so they *look* for problems that are big or that occur often and then go about trying to remove them.

I used a similar approach when I arrived at KFC in 1994, when we faced multiple challenges. One of the first steps I took was to attend regional franchisee meetings. At one meeting, an older, crustier franchisee stood up and said, "You better be good, son, because there's been a lot of guys like you to come through here." I was a little offended, but I also understood where he was coming from. The franchisees had seen plenty of corporate people do things that directly affected their livelihood—often negatively—and then move on to their next gig. I assured him, and others, that I wasn't going anywhere until we turned the company around. I was committed to solving the core problems, not slapping a few Band-Aids on and then hurrying away before they fell off.

There were nine regional franchisee meetings. At each one, I'd lay out what I had learned so far. Then I'd split up the franchisee members into groups of seven or eight and tell them to pretend that they were the president of KFC and to come back in an hour and tell me what their priorities were. Their responses—quality, new products, more training—were not surprising. We all understood what the problems were, but it was much more effective to ask the franchisees what they thought than to simply walk into their meetings and tell them what they needed to do. I was trying to do what Waze's Uri Levine emphasizes, which is talking to the people who are experiencing the problems to really understand them. With the franchisees, we developed an action plan. We went from "me" to "we." I shared how we solved KFC's problems in chapter 16, and I'll repeat what I wrote there: what ultimately turned KFC around was a triumph of human spirit because we only began generating or discovering ideas for new products once we started working together on the problems rather than point fingers and avoid them.

One of the best benefits of tackling big problems is that you get to experience a world without that problem in it, even if only for a while, or even if only for a group of people. It's incredibly motivating to make problems go away. Helping someone with a problem is a learning opportunity. When we decided to tackle hunger at Yum!, we learned so much about how to best donate money and time to create the greatest impact and to keep our employees inspired to contribute however they could. We tied into the World Food Programme, we volunteered all around the world, and we used our restaurants to build awareness of hunger. In Louisville, Kentucky, 40 percent of kids go to bed hungry, so the Lift a Life Novak Family Foundation supports the Dare to Care Food Bank. We know that our efforts aren't going to eradicate hunger for everybody, in all communities. But we learn with every effort that solves the problem for at least some people, and that's worthwhile. Who knows how that learning might eradicate the problem in other communities in the future.

The best way to convince yourself to tackle problems is to look at them as the learning opportunities that they are. The bigger the problem, the more you'll learn by tackling it. Just think about what scientists, even the whole nation, learned as a result of trying to solve the problem of how to get a man on the moon.

More than likely, there's a problem lurking nearby in your life or work. Find it and dive in.

Learning by Tackling Problems

- What's one of the biggest problems you've tackled in your life or career? What did you learn from the process in terms of self-knowledge, new skills, or character strengths? How did that learning help you moving forward?

- Where do you feel stuck in your work or life? Have you done a problem-detection study to pinpoint the root problem? What would that process look like given the circumstances? What questions would you ask, and of whom?

- Is there a problem you're avoiding right now? What's holding you back from trying to solve it? Have you considered how solving it might benefit others, because that could be the source of your motivation to try?

Learn by simplifying

Chapter 24

Duckies and Goats

My daughter, Ashley, was born two-and-a-half months premature and weighed 4 pounds, 10 ounces. The doctors warned us about possible complications from premature birth, and even told us that she might not make it at all. When I first saw her, though, all I could think was how beautiful she was. I reached down to touch her with my finger, which she immediately grabbed and squeezed. Right then, I knew she was going to live.

I stayed with her and Wendy as they both overcame the complications that resulted from Wendy's diabetes. Wendy lost much of her sight for months (fixed eventually through laser surgery). I focused on staying positive, doing everything in my power to make sure Ashley made it through.

I was told her lungs, brain, and heart still had to develop, but I thought that there must be something more we could do to facilitate the process. I asked, "What will keep her alive?" The doctors told us that studies had shown that the more we could be with her, the more likely she was to survive. Constant contact mattered, they said, and hearing our voices. (Recent science proves this. Preemies who get skin-to-skin contact fare much better, and so do babies who hear their mother's voice more, even from recordings.[1])

Wendy and I spent every minute we could with her in the neonatal intensive care unit. When we had to sleep, we asked the nurses to play recordings we had made on a tape player we brought in so that Ashley would know she wasn't alone. When she was finally opening her eyes for longer stretches, I asked, "What color will she be able to see?" They told me red, so I bought her a red happy apple with a smile painted on its face.

She made it, of course, and as she got older, it became our ritual at bedtime for her to squeeze my finger when I tucked her in for the night. On her wedding day, she grabbed my finger and gave it a squeeze just as I gave her away, sending me back to my seat weeping. Ashley's happy apple now sits on a shelf in her own kids' room.

Throughout my life, I've employed the same strategy I used to learn what I could do to keep my daughter alive: **I ask the simplest question possible to get to the most important and insightful answer.** When I was trying to decide whether to hire someone and all the other criteria had been met, I would always ask myself one simple question, "Would I want Ashley to work for this person?" When I was trying to figure out how to grow or improve a team or a business, I would ask those I was leading, "What would you do if you were me?" Or I would ask myself, "If some hotshot came in and took over for me, what would they do?" In marketing, over and over I would ask, "What one perception, belief, or habit do we have to shift or build to grow the business?" When my teams have answered that question succinctly, we almost always hit paydirt. (For instance, Taco Bell helped change the hamburger habit by getting customers to, as our ad campaign put it, "think outside the bun," which really rung the register for the brand.)

Simple questions were the most direct path to the essential truths and valuable information I needed to learn. But that wouldn't have been possible if I hadn't first *simplified the issue.* **It's hard to ask a simple question if you haven't brought the issue down to its simplest form.** With Ashley's situation at birth, for example, there were a lot of complicated medical and biological challenges. But in its simplest form, the issue was life or death.

Not all issues are so stark or dire, but they can be reduced to a simple essence. Like jewelry-mogul Kendra Scott's famous "Sister Rule" for customer service: What would you do if the customer were your sister (or brother)?

Active learners know that the fastest way to start learning is to simplify. It's a virtuous cycle: **active learners take the time to simplify so that they can learn, which allows them to take the time to learn so that they can simplify.** What they're learning is the most *essential* information, which helps them take the most effective action.

Some years ago, John Maeda, an artist, product designer, and MBA student at MIT who founded the MIT SIMPLICITY Consortium, wrote a wonderful and simple book called *The Laws of Simplicity*, sharing ten laws in a hundred pages. Law four was "Learn":

> Operating a screw is deceptively simple. Just mate the grooves atop the screw's head to the appropriate tip—slotted or Phillips—of a screwdriver. What happens next is not as simple, as you may have noted while observing a child or a woefully sheltered adult turning the screwdriver in the wrong direction. . . . So while the screw is a simple design, you need to know which way to turn it. *Knowledge makes everything simpler.* This is true for any object, no matter how difficult. The problem with taking time to learn a task is that you often feel you are wasting time, a violation of the third Law ["Time"]. We are well aware of the dive-in-head-first approach—"I don't need the instructions, let me just do it." But in fact this method often takes longer than following the directions in the manual.[2]

Getting to simplicity on the far side of complexity takes time, effort, and intention, but active learners know that time is well worth it.

Whenever I was trying to get to the root of an issue, communicate vital information, or learn something critical, I tried to "make it duckies and goats"—my phrase for keeping it simple. It came from the children's books I read to Ashley, which were usually short and about cute animals like duckies and goats. It wasn't lost on me that these books were engaging and memorable and made complex ideas digestible. Compare that to what we usually see in life and business as adults—complicated reports, impossible-to-follow instructions, health regimens that will never hold up to the challenges of real life.

I have watched CEOs spend millions of dollars on consultants because they didn't take the time to simplify their business, challenges, or opportunities. PepsiCo had consultants crawling around in every department. To me, it seemed like such a waste because the leaders hadn't even simply defined what the real problem was. They didn't know what they wanted or needed from the consultants. They were just there, trying to prove their value. And just like businesses, I've watched people struggle, feel anxious, and lose ground because they didn't take the time to simplify what they needed or what they needed to do.

I think it's important to make the effort to simplify in three key areas:

First, **simplify your strategy, purpose, or mission.** There's nothing more liberating than a tight strategy; it gives you absolute clarity about what you need to do next. I made sure all our strategies were simple and unambiguous, that they could be interpreted only *one* way. People were clear on what success looked like and how to achieve it. We learn faster when we're not wasting time moving in the wrong direction. When I left Yum!, I took time to simplify my essential purpose—make the world a better place by developing better leaders—so that I was absolutely clear what I should be doing day by day. By letting it guide me, I've been able to learn more of the most important things.

Second, **simplify your communication.** In high school, I became the editor of the school newspaper. I loved it so much I decided to study journalism in college, which taught me to simplify how I communicate, because that's what journalists do: use the fewest possible words to communicate the most essential information in a way that anyone can understand.

Simple communication doesn't mean boring communication, though. Simple is often how you can break through the clutter. Whether you're building an advertising campaign, trying to get a message through twenty layers of management, or figuring out how to talk to your kids about cleaning their rooms or dating, you've got to find a way to be engaging and memorable, like duckies and goats.

I did that with my high school paper when I wrote an editorial criticizing the coaching of our basketball team, one of the best teams in the state that never seemed to win a championship. You weren't supposed to criticize any member of the faculty, especially a coach who had been there for years. But it got people's attention.

That training in simple, clear communication continued in my time working for Tom James at the ad firm Ketchum, McLeod, & Grove, when I was twenty-five. He had me rewrite test-market analysis memos six or seven times until I could put forth a recommendation and explain the rationale for that recommendation in just one page. I've tried to force myself to use this same discipline ever since, because it helps me clarify and, in the process, *learn* what I'm trying to convey. It cuts through the clutter in my own mind by forcing me to strip away the unnecessary and the irrelevant.

When I went to Warren Buffett for advice on communicating with Wall Street analysts, he pointed me to his own Berkshire Hathaway annual reports, which are so legendary they've become collector's items. Here's how he explained his approach to me: "I talk to our owners and potential owners like I would to my sister, Bertie. Bertie is very intelligent, but she doesn't know our business. So, I start out with a silent 'Dear Bertie,' then I write in plain English what I think she would want to know: here's where we are; here's where we want to be; here's how you can measure us; and here's how it's going to work for you." I thought of the investors as people who knew more than me, but Warren reminded me that they didn't, at least not when it came to my company. I sent him a copy of my next annual report, written with his principles of simplicity and clarity in mind, and he wrote back, "Bertie would be proud of you." I hung the note in my office as a reminder to keep things simple.

Third, **simplify the situation, circumstances, or approach down to the essentials of success.** Take the time to understand the fundamentals of whatever you're doing and check yourself against them.

Every business turnaround I've been a part of required the company to get back to the basics: quality, value, service, operations, and innovation or improvement. The first thing most leaders want to do in these situations is make an immediate impact, so they gravitate toward the broadly visible stuff like a new advertising campaign or sales promotion. But I learned it was more important to simplify the situation first and get the fundamentals right. During my first few months as Pepsi's COO in 1992, we focused on getting the trucks out of the warehouse efficiently and making sure there was enough product on the trucks when they left. Basic stuff you're not going to put in a commercial. When I helped turn around KFC in 1990 and Pizza Hut in 1993, they had both lost sight of quality. Pizza Hut had reduced the toppings it used, and KFC had stopped marinating its chicken. Somewhere along the way leaders had lost sight of fundamentals. New marketing initiatives are sexy and can give sales a boost, but if you don't put enough pepperoni on the pizza, it doesn't matter how cool your commercial is. You won't succeed in the long run.

The worst thing you can do to a business is add complexity that doesn't increase sales. **If you're struggling, simplify and focus on the fundamentals. Compare what you're working on to those fundamentals. Are you moving closer to them or further away?**

Chik-fil-A does this well, starting with the product that built the foundation for its business—a really good chicken filet sandwich. By staying focused on the basics of quality and service, the teams there learn how to do those basics better than anybody else.

Consequently, the company's volumes are three times higher than anybody else's.

John Meada likes to say, "Simplicity = Sanity." Eric Yuan, the founder of Zoom, seemed to understand that concept at its core. Zoom was created to solve a complaint that people had about most other videoconferencing tools: complexity. He wanted to make Zoom as simple to use as possible, looking at some of the great simplifiers like Google and Apple for inspiration. But he also wanted to carry that simplicity into how the company operated, how it priced its products, and on and on. He told me that "on day one, I told our team and myself as well, let's make sure every day before we have a process, let us think about how to simplify the process." He wanted to avoid establishing processes too quickly, which leads to unnecessary complexity and unhappy employees or customers, and, usually, backtracking to simplify the processes. "I think that's too late," he said.* Because you've already made people *un*happy. The process of simplifying from the start helped them learn what was essential to meeting the needs of employees and customers, and that's been key to their success.

In his book *Essentialism*, Greg McKeown explains that essentialists are explorers who "evaluate a broad set of options before committing to any. Because Essentialists will commit and 'go big' on only the vital few ideas or activities, they explore more options at first to ensure they pick the right one later."[3] Those *vital few* are the fundamentals or basics each of us needs to live a happy, fulfilled, successful life. As soon as we overcomplicate our lives and lose touch with them, we feel less happy, less successful, and less fulfilled.

Learning itself is a method of simplifying all the information that comes at us so that we can absorb it, process it, and then take the

* Note that Eric's first language is not English, so I have edited these quotes slightly for clarity.

right action. But when we do the work intentionally, when we *make the effort* to simplify whenever we bump up against complexity in life, we learn more and we learn faster.

Learning by Simplifying

- What have you learned in the past when you took the time to simplify something that seemed overly complex? What have you learned by trying to understand the fundamentals of a business, process, or situation?

- What methods do you use to make your communication as simple and engaging as possible? For instance, how many times do you reread an important email before you send it? When you make the effort to simplify, do you find that you understand what you're trying to communicate better?

- What feels too complex in your work or life right now? Where do things feel slow, sluggish, or difficult? What strategies could you use to start simplifying?

Chapter 25

No Hoarding Allowed

Learn by teaching

Katy Milkman's book, *How to Change*, includes a great bit of contrarian wisdom: giving advice is more helpful than getting it.

In one study, Milkman and her colleagues asked high schoolers to give students in lower grades advice on how to be successful. Most of the advice they gave was advice they'd received themselves—develop good study habits, don't procrastinate, and so forth. "Lo and behold, our strategy worked," she wrote.[1] "The students who had given just a few minutes of advice performed better. . . . [It] didn't turn C students into valedictorians, but it did boost performance for high schoolers from every walk of life."

Active learners understand that we learn by sharing what we know with others. They are super spreaders of ideas, knowledge, skills, and insights. It feeds their desire to learn, and it brings fulfillment and joy. Even many of the young people in Milkman's study asked if they could do it again.

This sense of joy in teaching has been a guiding light in my work and life. If you had asked me what I wanted to be when I grew up when I was a kid moving from town to town with my family, I would have said, "Baseball player or teacher." I was wrong about baseball, of course, but as I rose into leadership positions and spent more time helping people grow and achieve, I discovered I had in some ways become a teacher.

You might be thinking, "That's not what he told us about his purpose a few chapters ago." That's true. I've shared my passion for *leadership* throughout this book. But teaching and leadership are intertwined. To be a great leader, you *must* pass on what you learn to others, and that's the aspect of leadership I've enjoyed the most. Giving the gift of our knowledge and experience to others is the most gratifying and rewarding thing of all. And you get the added benefit of learning so much by doing it.

Timo Boldt, founder of the highly successful British meal kit company Gousto, told me about his experience as he began speaking at conferences and giving guest lectures for MBA students: "If you're forced to distill your thoughts on a piece of paper, and you have to write it down, and you know the audience is really educated and sophisticated and you can't just wing it, it's amazing how it helps you learn what you already know."

Two things happen in the brain that help us "learn what we know." One is that we believe ideas more when we share them with others verbally, especially if we're trying to convince others that they're true. Psychologists call it the "saying is believing effect." Want to convince yourself to make time to exercise three times a week? Try convincing somebody else that they could fit a simple exercise regimen into their schedule. Another is that speaking (and writing) brings a different part of our brain into play than just thinking, which changes how we think about an idea. It's one reason that we can struggle and struggle to come up with a solution to a problem, but almost as soon as we explain the problem to another person out loud, a good solution pops into our head. Talking it out forces us to slow down, zoom out (simplify), and order our thoughts.

Once while I was at PepsiCo, Roger Enrico called me into his office and said, "David, I know you have all these theories about building teams that make big things happen, and they seem to be working. I'd like you to put together a program you can teach to our high-potential leaders." To be clear, many of my "theories" were proven insights I had gathered from other experts, from my own mentors and teachers, and from more than a decade of experience as a leader to that point. Still, I considered it a real compliment and was thrilled to have the assignment.

The process of creating the course, of codifying what I believed about good leadership, was a powerful learning experience. Authors and speakers will tell you that building a curriculum or any teaching content pushes you to question every idea you include. Is it true? Can I prove it or support it? Does it make sense? Is it really the best idea? How does it fit with the other ideas? This deep analysis forces you to let go of ideas that aren't valid or essential and dig deep on the ones that are. It forces you to focus and reflect more than you are probably used to or comfortable with. (And for authors, it's really an act of courage, because the book stands alone, without you there to talk it up or explain it. It's why I admire authors so much.)

I learned things I didn't know, *and* I learned what I already knew, as Timo put it, as I analyzed leadership, considered it from different angles, and expanded or supported my ideas. **Active learners use this process to codify their ideas into something digestible and easily shared.** When you codify it, you can scale it. Why do you think Coach John Wooden came up with his now-famous pyramid of success?

Teaching well also forces you to stay on top of your game, to continually look for new material to keep your ideas current and relevant. And it forces you to learn good storytelling, an invaluable skill. Stories are stickier than almost any other kind of information. If you want an idea to stay with people, you better be able to convey it in a relevant, compelling story with emotion and tension.

I worked hard to create a leadership class that I hoped would not only inform but inspire and entertain, and I was looking forward to the opportunity to share it with my colleagues at PepsiCo. But I never got the chance. The news that the restaurant division was being spun off (to eventually become Yum! Brands) came the week before my first scheduled seminar, so I canceled it. I didn't want all my hard work to go to waste, though, so I began thinking about how to use the program at Yum!

Jack Welch was a business legend, and shortly before Yum!'s launch in 1997, Andy Pearson arranged for me to meet him. Over lunch, after I had furiously scribbled down two hours' worth of notes, I asked him one last question: "If you were me, what would be the single most important thing you'd focus on?"

"You know," Jack said, "when I think back to my early GE days, one of the things I wish I had done was talk more about who we wanted to be, what our values were, how we were going to work together, and how we were going to define ourselves as a company." This one sentence validated everything I had been thinking. I wanted to make our company special, a dynasty, and I wanted to spread that gospel. I decided to use the leadership program, which I called "Taking People with You," as a vehicle for helping people understand our vision, strategy, goals, and culture—especially our culture. I was almost glad I never got the chance to deliver it at PepsiCo. Now I could deliver it to our own people and tailor it to the restaurant business to build our new, unique company.

The first time I taught the Taking People with You program, my audience was just eight European general managers in a London hotel conference room. Over the years since, I've presented it to more than four thousand people on five continents. It has become the foundation of much of the work we do at David Novak Leadership and at Lift a Life.

The seminar evolved as I learned more about how to refine the ideas, make the presentation tighter, and make it more engaging. Three days were trimmed down to two. At times, I thought about modularizing it so that other people within the company could present it, but I loved teaching it and delivering it personally, which was sometimes more important than the content itself. First, I was sharing leadership lessons from experts I had consulted with directly, and that gave the ideas more credibility. People felt like the ideas were unfiltered, just one degree of separation away from the origin. Second, it gave people a chance to put a face to a name, to hear about my personal successes and failures, and to spend real time with me. That so many people throughout the company had a chance to get to know me and feel comfortable talking with me seemed fundamental to our culture.

I knew that part of what made it special and powerful is that I, as CEO, was teaching it. I was often asked how I could justify spending so much of my time on it, given all my other responsibilities. I said that it was the most effective and efficient thing I could do because our people saw that I was living the ideas and values I was sharing, and that inspired them to do the same. It also sent a subliminal message: "If our CEO devotes so much of his time teaching all this stuff about teamwork and leadership, it must be important."

Eventually, though, I needed to scale the ideas and make them accessible to everybody in the company, so I turned it into a book, *Taking People with You: The Only Way to Make Big Things Happen.*

Bill Harrison felt the same about his own leadership program at JPMorgan Chase. A big part of culture building, he told me, "is bringing people together through teamwork and partnership and getting them to understand strategy and understand the issues and talk about them." It was work he loved doing as a leader, but it became especially important when JP Morgan & Co. and Chase Manhattan Bank merged in 2000. "When you're bringing two strong banks together, it's really important to bring people together. So I started a leadership program." The course was taught for two days every month for two straight years as the companies merged. Bill acted as emcee and taught some of the sessions. He also brought in outside support. I was on the board of the company at the time and got a chance to teach my program on the power of recognition. "It was a great way to connect with everybody and build our culture," Bill said.

What I came to understand better with programs like these is that **you don't only learn about your own ideas; you learn new ideas**

from the people you're teaching. Of course, that's only possible if you approach teaching as a discussion, not a lecture. I've told the story of Andy Pearson getting horrible reviews after his first semester teaching Harvard MBA students. "They said I wasn't teaching," he told me. "They said I was preaching." In my enthusiasm, I can get preachy, too, so I purposefully structured much of my program as a discussion group and question-and-answer session rather than a one-way presentation. I made it a requirement that every participant bring an idea or project they were working on that they believed would have the biggest impact on our growth. I got to learn about those ideas and coach people on how to get them accomplished. It's as Rabbi Chanina said all the way back in the first century: "I have learned much from my teachers, more from my colleagues, and most from my students."[2]

I often reassessed my ideas based on the questions people asked me during programs. For instance, one of the original ideas I covered was, "Some people will say it can't be done every step of the way." But when an attendee asked, "What if they're right?" it made me reevaluate. It was a valid question. I started pairing the idea of having conviction with the lesson, "Understand and overcome the barriers to success."

The Q&A I used in my seminar was just my version of the Socratic method—using a series of provocative questions to encourage the listener to come to their own conclusions. That's why there are questions at the end of each chapter in this book. I pushed for this approach in our training. Just the corporate world's use of the word *training* illustrates the problem. It implies a kind of rote monkey-see-monkey-do process as opposed to real *learning*, where the emphasis is on engaging and involving the listener. What spread in our culture was know-how sharing through discussion-oriented programs.

Teaching also helps you learn *about* your audience, and that's how you build your connection with larger groups. Bobbi Brown, the renowned makeup artist and entrepreneur, has developed nine books and a master class on her craft. She was the beauty editor on the *Today* show for fourteen years, doing monthly educational segments. She's done so much teaching and believes she is a good teacher because she has developed compassion and empathy for her audience over the years. She understands people's struggles with self-image and confidence and has a genuine desire to help.

Your capacity to teach is only as great as your capacity to learn, *and* I can't think of a person I would call a real active learner who doesn't spend time teaching, partly because it's just so rewarding. The part I love best about teaching isn't the act of teaching itself. It's discovering how people use the ideas to make a difference. At Yum! it was that magical moment at the end of the day when everyone got together in informal groups and talked about what they were going to do differently next week. Or the responses I received when I followed up with people after the program to find out how they were putting the lessons into practice and how they were being active in their learning.

Any teacher will tell you that there's no greater joy than when something you say or do inspires people to examine their behaviors, ideas, thinking, and habits—when maybe, in some small way, you made a difference in their lives. I hope you get to experience that same joy and learn powerful lessons from your own students.

Learning by Teaching

- Have you ever had to figure out how to teach an idea, approach, or process to somebody? If so,

    - How did your understanding of or clarity about the thing you were teaching change?

    - What did you learn from the person or people you were teaching? Maybe from the questions they asked or the examples they shared?

- Is there something you're struggling to learn or make stick in your life or work? Is there somebody you could teach it to?

No Lip Service

Learn by making everyone count

While I was working on this book, my wife, Wendy, suffered a stroke.

A few months before, a sustained drop in her blood sugar had led to a severe seizure, which for someone with diabetes can be a near-fatal event. That seizure caused a cascade of other health issues and eventually the stroke.

After the stroke, I found myself crying at night, on the golf course, just walking around the house. I thought I was losing my wife, my partner, the love of my life. One day, I got a call from Ken Langone, one of the cofounders of the Home Depot and a friend and mentor for years. He's known for being tough, brash, and loud, all words he would use to describe himself. But that day, he knew I was down and struggling. "David," he said, "I'm going to come take you for a ride. We'll go get an ice cream." So we went to a Dairy Queen and sat in the drive-through line talking. He told me that when he was a kid, his father used to take him to Dairy Queen when he had had a tough day. Things just seem better when you have ice cream, his dad told him. It was a kind gesture that meant something to him, and he thought it would mean something to me. It was the best ice cream I've ever had.

Ken is a man who could give you anything—almost literally—but I learned from him that a kind gesture and a listening ear are the most valuable gifts. I felt supported and loved. I felt like I counted to him. It helped me rekindle my hope and optimism. Wendy, after hard work and the gift of time, came back from the stroke, and I was better able to support her on the journey because of what Ken and other people in my life did for me.

Active learners understand that people—not knowledge or results—should be the priority. How we support people, how we show our gratitude for them, how we show our interest or concern for them has a much greater impact, especially over time, than the latest quarterly earnings or the latest market rankings. I've said it before: I really like to win. But you don't win for long if the people who make the winning possible don't know how much they count.

We hear this advice so often it becomes white noise. Put people first. It seems obvious, common sense. But like most good advice, being obvious doesn't make it easy and doesn't mean people follow it. People and companies are good at giving lip service to the idea. But how often are they showing people that they're a priority through their actions, the way Ken did for me.

Active learners focus on building deep, positive relationships. Peter Senge, the brilliant systems thinker and expert on the concept of personal mastery, has explained that "[p]eople with a high sense of personal mastery . . . feel connected to others and to life itself."[1] They feel this way because they live in a "continual learning mode." They're curious about other people, which grows their empathy, compassion, and ability to look at situations from another's perspective. Active learners know those strengths will lead to more learning and greater fulfillment.

Focusing on people helps you learn more about the world around you—*and* gain a better understanding of yourself. You discover how to be vulnerable, which encourages people to be vulnerable back, to share ideas and insights that they might not have otherwise. These can be the ideas and insights that matter the most because they're not necessarily *easy*. They're not *surface*.

I have always admired Geoff Colvin, senior editor-at-large of *Fortune* magazine and author of books like *Talent Is Overrated* and *Humans Are Underrated*. When he joined me on my podcast, he described the kinds of high-value work that only humans can do and that technology or AI can't: empathy, collaboration, and the insights or learning we generate along the way. In *Humans Are Underrated*, he shared research published in the *Journal of Neuroscience* on the brain benefits of spending time with others: "When two people talk to one another face-to-face, their brains synchronize. . . . The same regions light up at the same time."[2] And as they read each other's body language and facial expressions and try to understand the other person's thinking, their executive functioning gets more exercise.

Executive functioning is our highest-level thinking, or how we solve problems, control our impulses, respond appropriately in certain situations, plan, analyze, strategize, assess, and more. It's how we go about achieving our goals in the world. "Together in person, face-to-face, we become literally smarter and more capable as a group," Geoff wrote, and "it can also make each of us smarter individually in important ways. . . . Just having an in-person conversation is such an intense, fully engaging experience that it builds our highest overall mental abilities."

Carol Tomé, the CEO of UPS, learned this lesson the hard way early in her leadership career. Carol had a woman on her team with potential, but who was struggling. She needed coaching. "I didn't want to do it," Carol told me. "I didn't understand the importance of leadership that's about investing in people and putting them first." Instead of coaching the struggling employee along the way, Carol waited to share a rough performance review with the employee, which she did over the phone. "Well, you can imagine what she did: she quit," Carol said. "And do you blame her? Of course not. But what was in my face is that she didn't quit the company; she quit *me*. She quit me because I was a bad leader. So I vowed on that day, from that moment on, nobody would ever quit me again. If they left me, they were leaving me because it was a great opportunity. Or they were going to leave me because it was time for them to go retire or the job wasn't right for them. But no one was going to quit me. And since that incident . . . I am laser focused on putting people first."

I was forced to learn this at a young age. When we arrived in each new town, I knew I was just one friend away from happiness, from discovering fun and excitement, from making the most of my time there. That experience and my parent's example helped develop my focus on people, and it's a big source of pride that I've been able to help others develop it too.

When Andy Pearson and I teamed up to launch Yum!, I knew that I would learn a lot from him. He had been a senior director at McKinsey & Company, and then he had helped take PepsiCo from a $1 billion to a multibillion-dollar juggernaut. After that, he taught at Harvard Business School before moving on to work for the leveraged-buyout firm Clayton, Dubilier & Rice, which is where he was right before Yum!

Andy also had a tough-as-nails reputation. In 1980 he had been a subject of one of the most famous articles in *Fortune* magazine's history: "The Ten Toughest Bosses to Work for in America." It was one of those distinctions that could be taken two different ways, but Andy was so proud of it, he hung the article up in his office.

What I didn't understand early on is just how important Andy would become in my life as a mentor and one of my very best friends, *or* how much Andy would learn from me. We constantly traded ideas about leadership, and I talked to him about what I thought we could achieve by creating a culture that makes people want to come to work every day. I think it rubbed off on him. A couple of years into our time at Yum!, he said to me, "There's a powerful human yearning for a certain amount of toughness and discipline." This was the old Andy, the tough boss. But then he added, "But it has to be balanced with a genuine concern for the other person. There's a big difference between being tough and being tough-minded." I did a mental double take. He had clearly seen the proof in our performance, but more than that, he was a deep lifelong learner, and I think he discovered how much more he could learn in the people-centric culture we were building. The kicker came in 2001 when Andy was the subject of another magazine profile, this one in *Fast Company,* titled, "Andy Pearson Finds Love."

Too many leaders and organizations set their priorities out of order: they're so focused on making money and beating the competition that their people take a backseat. **First, you support your team's capabilities, then you all learn together how to satisfy more customers, and *then* you make money. This is my long-held formula for success,** the idea that I repeated at Yum! every day in my words and actions: *everyone* counts.

Junior Bridgeman takes this idea to the extreme. While building a successful career as a player for the NBA, he also built a career in the food industry, investing in Wendy's franchises. Today, he owns hundreds of restaurants, Coca-Cola bottling plants, and *Ebony* and *Jet* magazines. As a franchisee, he turned around multiple struggling markets. When I asked him how, he just said, "It's always about the people."

Early on in his career, he did what most new owners did: he got new people. One store had turned over every employee three times before Junior started to see that if he wanted people to care about the store and the company, he had to show that he cared about *them.*

Some of the first restaurants Junior owned were in Milwaukee. At the time, if you were stopped for a traffic violation there, you were often taken directly to jail. His employees usually didn't have the money to bail themselves out. So, when an employee was stuck in jail and couldn't come to work, Junior and his team bailed them out. Slowly, **those kinds of actions, of helping employees when they fell on hard times, proved that the company cared about its people. Then the people started to care back.** And as they did, the restaurants became more and more successful.

Aneel Bhusri, one of the cofounders and CEO of Workday, an enterprise management software company that competes with industry behemoths, shares the same belief as Junior Bridgeman. "We're up against these really formidable companies," he explained. "We've got a great idea. We've got disruptive technology. But we need the best people." People were Workday's competitive advantage, so he personally interviewed the first *five hundred* people the company hired. He was specifically looking for signs that a person was aligned with the company's values and culture and would commit to the company long term, and even that they had a sense of humor. (I've said elsewhere how important it is to have fun at work because you learn more when you do.) Those interviews took precedence over everything else he did. "We told those five hundred people, 'You're going to protect the culture and the value system.'"

By making people a priority, Aneel learned something about himself, as well. He was biased toward people from the "right" schools (a bias I've certainly bumped up against). "As it turns out," he said, "talent is everywhere. Sometimes you just have to look a little harder. And in some cases, the right schools didn't produce the best employees." He learned to look for people who wanted to succeed, were excited, and had done something interesting with their lives. Not many leaders, especially founders, put that kind of effort into building the best team.

It's equally true in our personal lives. I've talked about my love of golf in other chapters, but what I haven't explained is that one reason I love it so much is because you spend hours of uninterrupted time with friends on the course. I've built some of my closest friendships and partnerships there. It's a way for me to invest in my important and rewarding relationships.

Of course, *the* most important is my relationship with Wendy, and I do what I can to show her what our life together means to me. For instance, when our twenty-fifth wedding anniversary was approaching, I bought a large silver frame, had a print of the number 25 developed, and had a wide matte created to go around it. I put the matte on a conference table in my office for a month. I was still CEO of Yum! at the time. Whenever I thought of a special moment or experience Wendy and I had shared, I would go in and write it on the matte, as small as I could. I wrote "Harpo's on a Thursday night," our college hangout, and "The Beijing Olympics," which we were lucky enough to attend, and "The last ski run," because we loved to ski and would take the last run together at the end of each trip. At the end of the month, the matte was covered in memories. When I gave it to Wendy at our anniversary party, it was a thousand times more meaningful because it took time, focus, and care. And Wendy has given me the same in turn.

An absolute role model in putting people first is Jimmy Dunne. On September 11, 2001, Jimmy Dunne was on a golf course trying to qualify for the US Amateur Championship. Someone pulled him aside during the round, when he learned that more than a third of the people who work at his company, investment bank Sandler O'Neill and Partners, had died—sixty-six people, including his best friend.

Jimmy, as the surviving partner, helped lead the remaining team through a dark and difficult time. He made sure the company kept going, but he also took care of the families of those who had been lost. He made immediate, beyond-generous commitments. Every family continued to receive their loved one's salary for a year, plus bonuses. They were covered under the company's benefit plans for ten years.

Then Jimmy worked with a friend to set up a foundation that paid for college for all the children of his fallen colleagues. When an interviewer asked why they had gone so far to offer support, he said, "Because we believed that what we did would echo for a hundred years in the families of our people, their kids and their grandkids. . . . And that meant taking care of our people and their children with respect and reverence."[3] I've said that when you do the right things, the right things happen. I don't think I know of a better example. Jimmy's firm became one of the best on Wall Street (it merged with Piper Jaffray in 2020 to become Piper Sandler Companies), and I think it's because he showed the people who work there what they mean to him. Making people a priority pervades Jimmy's life. He operates with incredible empathy. Whatever he can do for a friend, he does. And because of this approach to the world, he learns important lessons every day that help him grow and expand his life and career.

If we don't show people that they are our priority through our words and actions, how will they know? What will they learn about us? And what learning will we *lose* if we lose our connection to them?

Learning by Making Everyone Count

- What's something you learned solely because of your connection to a person that you might have never learned any other way?

- How do you invest in your relationships or in your teams? How has it changed the way they engage with you?

- Who are some of the people in your life who you learn from almost daily? How do you show them that they're a priority?

Chapter 27

The Magic of a Floppy Chicken

Learn by recognizing on purpose

In my first job as a corporate leader, heading marketing at Pizza Hut, I led monthly department meetings where we traded knowledge, provided updates, and brainstormed solutions to problems. Oddly, no other department at Pizza Hut was doing this at the time, but for me, these meetings were the source of our best marketing and promotion ideas.

It was for those meetings that I created my first recognition award. I called it the Traveling Pan—a big silver pizza pan given monthly for a job well done. The recognized person's name was inscribed on the pan, added to the list of previous awardees. The "awarding of the pan" became our end-of-meeting ceremony, and everyone loved it. Even if we spent most of the meeting on some particularly difficult problem, everyone knew at least part of the meeting would be fun and uplifting.

The success of the Traveling Pan spurred me to make this kind of recognition a habit. I always thought it was a nice thing to do, and I loved seeing how it uplifted those who were recognized and their peers. But I don't think I truly understood the power of recognition until I became COO of Pepsi East.

At a roundtable meeting with about ten route salespeople at our St. Louis plant, I asked a question about what was and wasn't working in merchandising. Someone said, "Ask Bob about that. He really knows how to paint the store Pepsi." Someone else said, "Yeah, Bob showed me more in one afternoon than I learned my first year." And so on around the room: "Bob showed me this," "Bob showed me that," "Bob knows all about that." I looked over at Bob, who was a route salesperson like the others, and saw tears streaming down his face.

"Bob, people are heaping all this praise on you. Why are you so upset?"

"You know," Bob said, "I've been at this company for forty-seven years. I'm about to retire in a couple of weeks. And I never knew anybody felt this way about me."

Forty-seven years feeling completely unappreciated.

It hit me in the gut. I had seen the positive effect of recognition in other leadership positions, but that morning in St. Louis, I fully realized the critical and fundamental importance of recognizing the efforts of the people around you. I decided in that moment that I wanted to do everything I could to make sure we didn't have any more Bobs on my teams. I decided I would make recognition one of the key behaviors of my leadership. I wrote a book, *O Great One!*, about it. I created an online course to teach people how to do it well.

Our need to be recognized is so important and universal that in a commencement speech that she gave at Harvard, Oprah Winfrey, who has done more than 35,000 interviews over her lifetime, focused on it:

> As soon as that camera shuts off, everyone always turns to me and inevitably, in their own way, asks this question: "Was that OK?" I heard it from President Bush. I heard it from President Obama. I've heard it from heroes and from housewives. I've heard it from victims and perpetrators of crimes. I even heard it from Beyoncé in all of her Beyoncé-ness. . . . [We] all want to

know one thing: "Was that OK?" "Did you hear me?" "Do you see me?" "Did what I say mean anything to you?"[1]

The simple truth is that recognition matters to *all* of us. In a survey my company commissioned in 2016, *82 percent* of the participants indicated that they feel their supervisor doesn't recognize them enough, 43 percent wanted more recognition from their colleagues, and 60 percent said they are more motivated by recognition than by money, assuming they're paid enough to cover their bills.[2]

It doesn't matter whether you're dealing with a highly ranked executive or someone who's washing dishes in a restaurant, you can never underestimate the power of telling someone they're doing the right things well. The *right* things well. As a leader who is trying to drive certain behaviors and learn how to keep improving and growing along the way, recognition *on purpose* is more than a "nice to have." It's crucial. I learned early on that **recognizing *on* purpose and *with* purpose helps you encourage the behaviors that create a learning environment.**

A recognition culture became what Yum! was best known for. Companies visited us to learn how we did it and how we made it purposeful by tying it to behaviors we knew drove performance. If you want recognition to help you grow and succeed, you must first lay out what behaviors are key—so that's where we started. We called them our How We Work Together principles, which I shared in chapter 6. They weren't *values*, they were *behaviors*, and that was intentional. We leveraged what we learned from our best-practices tour of other companies, but we based the principles on the behaviors that were driving the success of our highest-performing restaurants. We uncovered them by studying the top 10 percent. Of course, recognition was one of the behaviors, because the managers saw that they got more of the positive behaviors that they recognized.

As our company grew, we focused on identifying behaviors that would take us to the next level. We wanted people to be know-how builders, spreading their knowledge and good ideas throughout the company. We also wanted to do a better job retaining talent. In the restaurant industry, especially quick-serve restaurants, turnover is high and the best talent is often needlessly lost. So we recognized leaders and managers who were people growers. We also knew we needed more big ideas and breakthroughs in our operations and product concepts, so we rewarded that behavior to ramp up innovative thinking.

Combined with the How We Work Together principles, the new ones we decided to reward and recognize became our How We *Win* Together principles. As we recognized them, we got more of them, and everybody in the company learned how to grow the business and grow their career by contributing in the best possible ways. We were encouraging them to learn by *doing*.

Purposeful recognition works because it shows people that you're watching, validates the person, and builds trust, because it demonstrates that you value their input and ideas. And then people are more engaged.

When people are more engaged, they're bringing more of their brain power to whatever is in front of them. Don't believe me? **Tomorrow, recognize a colleague, a team member, your spouse, or your kid for doing something that you've been trying to get better at doing. Then say, "How'd you get so good at that?" Stand back and wait for the wisdom.** I've already talked about the importance of asking good questions, but when you prime people's thinking with recognition, their answers become more revealing and powerful.

Doing recognition well requires practice. The best recognition by my experience, and research supports this, relies on a few basic principles:

- It should be earned, preferably based on something measurable or specifically defined. You should name the behavior you're recognizing.

- It should be authentic and from the heart.

- It should be personal to the giver and the receiver whenever possible.

- It should be spontaneous when possible. Catching someone by surprise—when they're least expecting it—adds to the impact.

- It should be *fun*.

- And it should be a part of how you operate or interact every day.

I learned these principles over a decades' long journey. **What I think made my efforts especially effective was that they were personal, spontaneous, and fun**.

I hadn't been at KFC that long when I learned that our head of information technology was recognizing people in his department by handing out those floppy rubber chickens you see in old comedy sketches. I liked the floppy chicken idea so much that in true presidential fashion, I stole it from him (with full permission and credit, of course).

I carried floppy chickens around in my briefcase (there's something not many corporate leaders would admit to). When I saw or heard about great behavior in a restaurant or an office, I'd introduce myself to the person and recognize their effort. "The general manager tells me you go above and beyond when serving customers," or "You're one of the best original recipe cooks I've seen." Then I said, "I've got to give you one of my floppy chickens." I'd pull it from my briefcase—often to astonished stares—write a personalized message on it, sign it, and number it (I gave away about a hundred a year). I'd have someone take a picture of the two of us, and I'd say, "We'll send you a copy, but the next time you're in Louisville, I want you to stop by so we can show you where your picture is hanging in my office. Because what you do matters." Finally, because they couldn't eat a rubber chicken, I'd hand the recipient a crisp $100.

And true to my word, I had hundreds of photos of people receiving the rubber chicken all over my walls. Eventually, we ran out of room on the walls, so we started hanging them on the ceiling, much to the chagrin of our loss-prevention team.

The more I did this, the more the word spread. It lit up the company. People cried when I gave them the rubber chicken, and so did the people watching. Some of the team members who worked in our restaurants had received very little positive feedback in their *lives*, never mind their work. The more I recognized people, the more the practice spread throughout leadership. The results for the company were unbelievable.

My success at KFC led to my role as CEO of Yum! Brands, but I often think, *What would have happened if I hadn't gotten the results at KFC?* I could imagine people saying, "Hey, you remember that guy David Novak, who was handing out floppy chickens while Rome was burning?" But those floppy chickens are the *reason* we got the results we did. I've always said that the KFC turnaround was a triumph of human spirit, and recognition was a huge part of making it possible.

The floppy chicken wasn't my first silly award or my last, because I was a silly award kind of guy. But I realize not everybody is, which is why making awards personal matters. After hearing my story of the power of recognition, Frank Blake, the former CEO of Home Depot, came up with the idea of handwritten notes, because that felt true to him. When he joined me on my podcast, he told me a funny but revealing story. During the week, the company had all its stores send in examples of great customer service. And every Sunday, Frank wrote many, many *handwritten* notes to those people, saying thank you for what they did and telling them that they were awesome.

At first, Frank wasn't sure if it was working. But after about three months, he was in a store and an associate approached him. "I got this note from you," the man said. "Would you mind sending me another copy?" Frank said, "No problem, but why?" The man said, "Well, we all looked at it and we figured it had to be RoboPen. You couldn't possibly have written it. So, we ran it under water to test it, and the ink ran. We ruined it." That's the power of personalization.

Fun and spontaneity matter, too—because they boost joy in the moment and create more memorable experiences. Without them, you get stale employee-of-the-month programs or onetime events that don't reflect the person, culture, or specific ways that individuals add value and show up as their best selves. When you see it, you should recognize it, especially because that's the moment when it could be the most meaningful. Wait, and you risk that person feeling unappreciated for weeks or months. And while they wait, do you think they're going to be super motivated to share their wisdom, knowledge, or good ideas?

John Wooden, for example, wanted to emphasize the power of "we" with the UCLA Bruins, so he established the expectation that anytime somebody scored a basket, whoever scored had to acknowledge the players who had helped. It could be as simple as pointing at the other player, but they needed to acknowledge the assist. When he told the team about the expectation, one of his players said, "Well, Coach, what if they're not looking?" Wooden replied, "Oh, they'll be looking." He knew how much that quick moment of recognition, at the time, would mean to every player on the team and the results the team produced together *in that game.* **If you don't want to wait for results to improve, don't wait to recognize the behaviors that produce the results.**

Yum! was a company full of fun, personalized awards given spontaneously for serious work—stars, smiley faces, boomerangs, magnets, crystal trophies, and silly walk-the-talk novelty chattering teeth. We were overflowing with smiles, applause, cheers, high fives, handshakes, thank-you notes, banners, kudos, and so much more. Some leaders gave out awards specific to their departments, like a mock *Time* magazine cover with the headshot of somebody who supported the company's PR efforts. We did all this because it was the most important way that we could express that we were a different kind of company, one that truly appreciated the contributions of its people. That's what other leaders came to us to understand.

We were recognized for this in 2013 when Geoff Colvin published an article in *Fortune* titled, "Great job! How Yum Brands Uses Recognition to Build Teams and Get Results," with a picture of the floppy chicken prominently featured.[3] It encouraged more companies to seek us out and learn from us, helping us to spread the power of recognition beyond our own walls.

Despite all this, I needed an occasional reminder to make recognition the priority it should be. With the pace of business today, it can be hard to pause and focus on celebrating. Once at Yum!, I was grinding out a presentation for an investor meeting the next day with my CFO, Rick Carucci (he later became president). Suddenly, we heard our roving recognition band—a group of volunteers who played instruments to literally trumpet their colleagues' success—coming down the hallway to celebrate an employee's contributions. Rick stood up, but I didn't. "We've got to get this presentation done," I said.

"David, this is what you're all about. If you're holed up in this office and you don't go out there, what kind of message does that send?"

I stood up, we went out, and I was immediately reminded that there, clapping, cheering, and watching the grinning celebrant turn red in the face, was the first place I *should* be, no matter what. What was fifteen minutes out of our afternoon compared to the great ideas this person might dream up and share with us going forward?

When I attended Yum!'s twenty-fifth anniversary celebration in 2022, six years after I stepped down as CEO, so many people came up to say wonderful things about our time working together. Everybody talked about the power of recognition. Just by doing that, they were recognizing *me*, and it not only made me feel great but made me feel confident that recognition was still a core behavior in the culture.

I know the widespread effect it is still having on the people at Yum! I know what a difference it made and is still making to the people who are recognized. I know the kind of behaviors it drives. I'm reminded of it over and over, but never more powerfully than when I attended the funeral for Chuck Grant, a talented engineer with KFC. Amazingly, I saw his floppy chicken at his side in his coffin. I had given it to him a few years before for an equipment innovation he had spearheaded. When I went to offer my condolences to his wife, she told me that before Chuck had died, he said that the one item he wanted placed in his coffin was his prized floppy chicken.

If that doesn't drive home the power of recognition, nothing will.

Learning by Recognizing on Purpose

- When was the last time you were recognized for a contribution? How did it feel? How did it make you want to contribute going forward?

- Have you worked in an environment or been part of a group or community where recognition was embedded in the culture? What was the environment like when it came to creative thinking or the open sharing of ideas?

- When was the last time you recognized somebody for their contribution? Did you take the time to ask them what prompted their thinking, idea, or action?

Conclusion

Masterpiece-
in-Progress

I like country music. I love its storytelling. I'm inspired by the songs of so many great artists, so much so that occasionally an idea for an opening line or a chorus will pop into my head, and I'll write it down.

Last year, Wendy and I celebrated our seventieth birthdays and our forty-eighth wedding anniversary. It was a big year and I wanted to do something truly special for Wendy. I decided I would finally do what I'd been thinking of doing since 1983—write a song for her.

I've been trained to be a writer for much of my life, but I've never written a song. If I wanted to do it well, I needed to *learn* how. I planned a trip to Nashville—because where else do you go to learn how to write country music—and booked a session with two songwriting greats: Jessi Alexander and Jon Randall.

I had an absolute blast. I learned so much about the music business, about how songwriters collaborate, and about how to put a song together. They helped me take the partial lyrics I had written way back in 1983, when I walked out of a sad movie thinking, *I'm glad I'm not sad about what I don't have, because I've got Wendy,* and turn them into an amazing song that captured so much of how I feel about Wendy and our life together. At the end of our session, they recorded it for me.

I had planned for the two songwriters to perform the song at our upcoming party as a surprise for Wendy. But when I got home from the airport, I couldn't wait to tell her. What if something happens to one of us, I thought, and she never hears this song. The next morning, I woke Wendy up and said, "I've got to be honest with you. I didn't go to Nashville on business." She looked startled. *Oh God, what did he do?*

I thought I should relieve her anxiety quickly. "I went to write you a song." And then I played it for her. By the last chorus of "I'll be damned if I'll be sad / If I lost everything I had . . . If it all went away today / I'd be OK cause I can say / I got Wendy," we were both crying. "This is the best day of my life," she said.

That's the power of learning: it elevates the impact you have on the people in your life and the world around you.

A few months later, on Christmas Eve, I opened my big present from Wendy. It was a guitar. "Geez, Wendy," I said, "I can't play the guitar. It's hard to learn the guitar, and I'm seventy years old."

And she said, "Hmm, that's not the David Novak I know"—again being my truth-teller. Wendy always keeps me open to new learning opportunities. So, I've taken the challenge and am learning to play the guitar. I don't suspect I'll ever be great at it, but that's not really the point. The point is to *learn*, to be disciplined about that learning, and to see where it takes me.

Warren Buffett once told me what he looks for in the companies he acquires. He said, "I'm looking to buy companies that are run by painters." When I asked for an explanation, he said, "Most great artists have a hard time letting go of their paintings. They're in love with the painting. They are constantly adding a dab of color here, a little more texture there. I'm looking for the boss who is always tweaking their company, constantly trying to make it better. No matter how successful they may have already been, what they still see is a masterpiece-in-progress." He calls Berkshire Hathaway a museum for these masterpieces, but he expects the people who run them to keep making progress, to keep changing and expanding.

That's the way I look at life. That's the way I look at business.

I had a few friends come visit not long ago. They'd never been to our home before, and I was giving them a tour. As we walked by our bedroom, they stuck their heads in, because we have a wonderful view from our window, and one of them started to laugh. "You've got a pillow on your bed that says *Dream Big!*" Yep, I do. They couldn't get over it.

I can understand their point. I have been enormously blessed. Most people looking at my life right now—what I've accomplished, how I live, my relationship with my family, my financial resources, and the fulfillment I get through the work of our foundation and our leadership company—would wonder what else I could possibly want. What "bigger" dream could I be hoping for?

But that's not the way I see it, or the way any active learner sees life. I'm proud of what I've accomplished in the past, I love what I do now, but there is plenty more to do, plenty more to learn. I'm sticking with the songwriting; I've written six now and I'm on my way to a full album. I recently became a partial owner of the Valhalla Golf Club in Louisville, where the 2024 PGA Championship will be played; I'm responsible for marketing, branding, and redesign of a one-of-a-kind Kentucky golf experience. That requires all sorts of learning. And, of course, we're constantly learning about how to expand our leadership education through the podcast, newsletter, courses, and more.

The active learning will never, never stop.

My life has always been full *and* I'm always dreaming about what's to come, because there's so much to learn. If I pursue it, I'll keep making life better, for me, the people I'm closest to, and the people I have the privilege to help, teach, or influence.

Active learners are painters. Artists. They see life as a masterpiece-in-progress, knowing that the more they learn, the more the masterpiece will reveal itself. Because as Frank Hubbard said, and the great John Wooden was fond of repeating, "It's what we learn after we think we know it all that counts."[1]

Notes

Introduction

1. Eric Hoffer, *Reflections on the Human Condition* (New York: Harper & Row, 1973).

Chapter 1

1. Dan McAdams et al., "Continuity and Change in the Life Story," *Journal of Personality* 74, no. 5 (October 2006), https://www.sesp.northwestern.edu/docs /publications/690081293490a093361fe6.pdf.
2. Tasha Eurich, *Insight* (New York: Crown Business, 2017), 146.

Chapter 2

1. Josh Waitzkin, *The Art of Learning* (New York: Free Press, 2007), 33.
2. Sukhinder Singh Cassidy, *Choose Possibility* (New York: Houghton Mifflin Harcourt, 2021), 51.
3. James Clear, "Motivation Is Overvalued. Environment Often Matters More," https://jamesclear.com/power-of-environment.

Chapter 4

1. N. Eisenberger, "The Pain of Social Disconnection: Examining the Shared Neural Underpinnings of Physical and Social Pain," *Nature Reviews Neuroscience* 1 (2012): 421–434.
2. G. M. Slavich et al., "Neural Sensitivity to Social Rejection Is Associated with Inflammatory Responses to Social Stress," *Proceedings of the National Academies of Science USA* 107, no. 33 (2010): 14817–14822.
3. Adam Grant, "What It Takes to Have Freedom and Psychological Safety at Work," *Granted*, October 2021, https://adamgrant.substack.com/p/616392_granted -october-2021.

Chapter 5

1. Sheryl Sandberg and Adam Grant, *Option B* (New York: Knopf, 2017), 16.
2. Patrick Anderson, "The Only Power Kissinger Has Is the Confidence of the President," *New York Times*, June 1, 1969.

Chapter 7

1. Carol Dweck, *Mindset* (New York: Random House, 2006), 3–4.
2. Erika Andersen, *Be Bad First* (New York: Bibliomotion, 2016), 3.

Chapter 8

1. Nancy Kline, *Time to Think* (London, UK: Cassell Orion, 1999), 15.

2. Adam Grant, *Think Again* (New York: Viking, 2021), 159–160.

Chapter 9

1. Nancy Kline, *Time to Think* (London, UK: Cassell Orion, 1999), 12.

2. Ting Zhang, Francesca Gino, and Joshua Margolis, "Does Could Lead to Good? On the Road to Moral Insight," *Academy of Management Journal* 61, no. 3 (2014), https://www.researchgate.net/publication/323750714_Does_Could_Lead _to_Good_On_the_Road_to_Moral_Insight.

Chapter 10

1. Stephen Klemich and Mara Klemich, *Above the Line* (New York: Harper Business, 2020), 55.

2. C. S. Lewis, *Surprised by Joy* (New York: HarperOne, [1955] 2017), 254.

Chapter 11

1. Ray Ginger, "Clarence Seward Darrow: 1857–1938," *Antioch Review* 13, no. 1 (1953): 60.

2. Clarence Darrow, *Sign Magazine,* May 1938.

3. Chip Heath and Dan Heath, *Decisive* (New York: Currency, 2013), 8. They were quoting Dan Lovallo and Olivier Sibony, "The Case for Behavioral Strategy," *McKinsey Quarterly* 2 (2010).

Chapter 12

1. Peter Georgescu, *The Source of Success* (San Francisco, CA: Jossey-Bass, 2005), 25–26.

2. Temple Grandin and Richard Panek, *The Autistic Brain* (New York: Mariner Books, 2013), 143–144.

Chapter 13

1. Galen Guengerich, *The Way of Gratitude* (New York: Random House, 2020), xi, 13.

2. Barbara Oakley, "Learning How to Learn," TEDx Oakland University, August 5, 2014, TEDx Talks, youtube.com/watch?v=O96fE1E-rf8.

Chapter 14

1. Stephen Klemich and Mara Klemich, *Above the Line* (New York: Harper Business, 2020), 89.

2. Martin Fladerer et al., "The Value of Speaking for 'Us': The Relationship between CEOs' Use of I- and We-Referencing Language and Subsequent Organizational Performance," *Journal of Business and Psychology* 36 (2021).

Chapter 16

1. Wikiquote, "Trust," wikiquote.org/wiki/Trust.

Chapter 17

1. Judy Willis, "The Neuroscience of Joyful Education," *Educational Leadership* 64 (Summer 2007), https://www.ascd.org/el/articles/the-neuroscience-of-joyful-education.

Chapter 18

1. Oscar Wilde, letter to Lord Alfred Douglas, *De Profundis,* 1905.
2. PwC, "What 52,000 People Think about Work Today: PwC's Global Workforce Hopes and Fears Survey 2022," May 24, 2022, www.pwc.com/gx/en/issues/workforce/hopes-and-fears-2022.html.
3. Pam Sherman, "Bringing the Character of You to Life's Stage," LinkedIn newsletter, October 6, 2023, www.linkedin.com/pulse/bringing-character-you-lifes-stage-pam-sherman/.

Chapter 19

1. William Samuelson and Richard Zeckhauser, "Status Quo Bias in Decision Making," *Journal of Risk and Uncertainty* 1 (1988).
2. Harvard University's Stress & Development Lab has free online resources to help you master cognitive reappraisal, available at https://sdlab.fas.harvard.edu/cognitive-reappraisal.
3. Adapted from Wendy Leshgold and Lisa McCarthy, *Fast Forward* (New York: Matt Holt Books, 2023), 28.

Chapter 20

1. Wendy Leshgold and Lisa McCarthy, *Fast Forward* (New York: Matt Holt Books, 2023), 208.
2. Brian Levenson, *Shift Your Mind* (New York: Disruption Books, 2020), 7.
3. Anders Ericsson and Robert Pool, *Peak* (New York: Houghton Mifflin, 2016), xxiii.

Chapter 21

1. Ryan Holiday, *Ego Is the Enemy* (New York: Portfolio, 2016), 56.
2. Charles L. Novak, *Home Is Everywhere* (New York: Disruption Books, 2018), 29.
3. David Rock, "How to Convince Yourself to Do Hard Things," *hbr.org,* December 7, 2021, https://hbr.org/2021/12/how-to-convince-yourself-to-do-hard-things.

Chapter 23

1. Daniel Lubetzky, *Do the KIND Thing* (New York: Ballantine Books, 2015), 33.

Chapter 24

1. Arvind Sehgal et al., "Impact of Skin-to-Skin Parent-Infant Care on Preterm Circulatory Physiology," *Journal of Pediatrics* (2020); Alexandra R. Webb et al., "Mother's Voice and Heartbeat Sounds Elicit Auditory Plasticity in the Human Brain before Full Gestation," *Proceedings of the National Academy of Sciences* 112, no. 10 (February 2015).

2. John Maeda, *The Laws of Simplicity* (Cambridge, MA: MIT Press, 2006), 33–34.

3. Greg McKeown, *Essentialism* (New York: Crown Business, 2014), 60.

Chapter 25

1. Katy Milkman, *How to Change* (New York: Penguin, 2021), 150.

2. Talmud, Ta'anit 7a.

Chapter 26

1. Peter Senge, *The Fifth Discipline* (New York: Crown Business, 2006), 132.

2. Geoff Colvin, *Humans Are Underrated* (New York: Portfolio, 2015), 63–66, based on research from Jing Jiang et al., "Neural Synchronization during Face-to-Face Communication," *Journal of Neuroscience* 32, no. 45 (November 7, 2012).

3. Brian Doyle, "Bank That Lost 66 Workers on 9/11 Has Paid for All Their Kids to Go to College," *Good News Network*, September 11, 2021, originally published in 2015.

Chapter 27

1. Oprah Winfrey, speech delivered for Harvard's 362nd Commencement, Tercentenary Theater, Cambridge, Massachusetts, May 30, 2013.

2. David Novak, "Recognizing Employees Is the Simplest Way to Improve Morale," *hbr.org*, May 9, 2016, https://hbr.org/2016/05/recognizing-employees-is-the-simplest-way-to-improve-morale#.

3. Geoff Colvin, "Great Job! How Yum Brands Uses Recognition to Build Teams and Get Results," *Fortune*, July 25, 2013, fortune.com/2013/07/25/great-job-how-yum-brands-uses-recognition-to-build-teams-and-get-results/.

Conclusion

1. Frank McKinney Hubbard (US humorist), *Fairmount News* [Indiana], February 17, 1913, per *The New Yale Book of Quotations*.

Index

Acknowledgments

First and foremost, I want to thank God. For the life of me, I will never know why I've been blessed with the life I have been given. I'm truly humbled by it and feel so thankful for my loving family, the joyful career experience I could never have dreamed of, and the exposure to many of the world's most successful and generous people.

The origin of this book stems from my daughter Ashley's encouragement for me to give back by sharing the learnings I have gleaned over the years. My heartfelt thanks go to all of you who have taken the time to invest in me and share your know-how. Your wisdom shines through on these pages, and I thank you all.

I can't overemphasize the absolute joy of working with Lari Bishop, who has helped me write this book. She is wicked smart, so creative, a great collaborator who worked tirelessly to put forward our best possible product. If you liked the framework and format of this book, she deserves most of the credit. Thanks as well goes to Tim Schurrer, who partners with me on the *How Leaders Lead with David Novak* podcast and helped identify the most impactful stories about how to learn. I also want to thank my literary agent, Jim Levine, and my editor, Scott Berinato. They pushed for excellence and added substantial value along the way. And thank you to the whole team at Harvard Business Review Press for your support and commitment along the way.

Last but not least, I want to thank my late mother, Jean Novak, who was my greatest teacher, and my wife, Wendy, who has been my truthteller and inspiration for what is possible if you never, ever give up.

Thank *you* for buying this book. All profits will go to the Wendy Novak Diabetes Institute to support our ongoing effort to help those inflicted with this devastating disease live a long, empowered life.

About the Authors

DAVID NOVAK is the founder of David Novak Leadership, a leadership development organization and platform, and the cofounder and former chairman and CEO of Yum! Brands, one of the world's largest restaurant companies, with over 1.5 million team members working in more than 135 countries.

His mission is to make the world a better place by developing better leaders.

He pursues this passion through courses, workshops, philanthropy, and especially his top-ranked podcast, *How Leaders Lead*, where he interviews high-profile leaders in business, sports, health care, and government. David is also the author of four leadership and personal development books: the *New York Times* bestseller *Taking People with You* (based on his original leadership development program), *Take Charge of You, O Great One! A Little Story about the Awesome Power of Recognition*, and *The Education of an Accidental CEO*.

David has been recognized as one of the world's top leaders by *Barron's*, *Fortune*, and *Harvard Business Review*, and was named CEO of the Year by *Chief Executive* magazine. During his tenure as CEO, Yum! Brands doubled in size, established itself as a global powerhouse, increased its market capitalization eightfold, and spun off Yum! China as an independent publicly traded company. Prior to leading Yum! Brands, he helped lead Pepsi-Cola, KFC, and Pizza Hut through major turnarounds, and held other senior management positions at PepsiCo divisions.

Through David Novak Leadership and the Lift a Life Novak Family Foundation, David founded the Novak Leadership Institute at his alma mater, the University of Missouri; runs Lead4Change, a leadership development and community service program for middle and high school students; and supports Global Game Changers, which helps pre-K through fifth-grade children develop self-esteem and confidence. The family foundation also focuses on the Wendy Novak Diabetes Institute and organizations that address food insecurity and early childhood education. In 2015, David received the prestigious Horatio Alger Award for his commitment to philanthropy and higher education.

David lives in North Palm Beach, Florida, with his wife, Wendy, who is the center of his world. He works with his daughter, Ashley Butler, executive director of the Lift a Life Novak Family Foundation, and is blessed with three grandchildren. He's an avid golfer, becoming Shinnecock Hill's oldest club champion at 69. He's currently writing country songs and learning to play the guitar.

· · ·

LARI BISHOP is a writer and editor who has collaborated on more than thirty books, including *New York Times* and *Wall Street Journal* best-sellers. She loves her work because every new project is a new learning experience.